FIFTY KEY WORDS IN THEOLOGY

LIST OF WORDS

INTRODUCTION

Fifty Key Words in Theology has been prepared as a brief, handy book of reference. It may also serve as a modest introduction to theological studies. The number and length of the articles have been governed by this dual aim.

The index shows that many terms have been explained which could not be treated in separate articles. The reader is encouraged to make full use of the index. Some terms have been omitted because they properly appear in other books in this series.

These brief articles may well serve as an elementary introduction to theological studies for the general reader. For example, one might begin with the article on "Theology". This would naturally suggest consulting the article on "Faith". Both would lead the reader to consult further articles until a useful acquaintance with major terms had been achieved.

The articles have been written from within one tradition of the Church Universal, but without ignoring other points of view. The teaching of theology in an ecumenical spirit does not mean discussing only views common to all the main schools of thought. It does mean a willingness to be addressed by all, and to take seriously what each has to say. It also means to be willing, in genuine charity, to speak back. The intention in all such dialogue is to be led more and more into the truth.

Mr Norman Healey, as a specialist in religious education, and my wife have helped by their comments in the preparation of the manuscript.

F. G. Healey

ANALOGY means partial likeness between two matters, whether beings or relationships, especially the kind of resemblance which makes further comparison between them possible. From the observation of a likeness, reasoning by analogy moves to the conviction that one of the two is also like the other in certain respects which are not observed, or cannot be observed. This method is used in theology to meet two problems which arise from the infinite disparity between God and what is not God (see 'Immanence and Transcendence').

The first has to do with man's knowledge about God. For example, from knowledge about the natural world and human nature, can we gain knowledge about God? Reasoning by analogy begins with the point that, from what a man makes and does, we do gain some knowledge about the man himself. From the fact of the physical universe and its characteristics, therefore, it is reasonable to deduce the power, the purposiveness, and so on, of God who made it. Again, from what we know of human nature, it is reasonable to infer that God as the maker of man is at least as personal as he.

The technical term for this line of argument is 'the analogy of being'. It is flatly rejected by some theologians. This is not because it is analogical but because, while professing to reach knowledge about God through reasoning alone, it is all the time making use of affirmations of faith (see 'Faith'). It is assuming the doctrine of creation, which they would say is a 'revealed' doctrine (see 'Revelation'). For the 'analogy of being', therefore, they would substitute the 'analogy of faith'.

The second problem has to do with human language about God. Words like goodness, wisdom, father, king, love, cannot be used of God in exactly the same way as they are used of human beings. That would be making God in the likeness of man. On the other hand, if God is utterly different from man, such words could not be used of him at all. Reasoning by analogy proceeds along the following lines. From what God has disclosed of himself (see 'Revelation'), it is plain that no such terms when applied to God could mean the same as when used of human beings. Nevertheless, between the revealed nature and activity of God on the one hand, and human nature and activity on the other, there is sufficient likeness to make such terms appropriate for expressing something essentially true about what God has shown himself to be and to be doing.

ATONEMENT is most frequently used in theology to signify the means whereby men are reconciled to God. It is sometimes used to denote the actual state of reconciliation with God.

The New Testament witnesses throughout to the fact of atonement by Jesus Christ. It includes more than one interpretation of the fact, however, and it is part of the task of theology to combine those various interpretations, as far as possible, in a coherent view. All the resulting theories of atonement agree that fellowship with God is man's highest good; that such fellowship is hindered or destroyed by sinfulness; and that it has become realizable through Jesus Christ. At different periods in the history of doctrine, however, some aspects of the Biblical testimony have been emphasized much more heavily than others.

For nearly a thousand years from the time of Irenaeus (about 130–200), the dominant theory explained the death of Christ in terms of a ransom paid to the Devil who, since the sin of Adam, had mankind in his power. The Devil was however deceived, and rendered powerless, because Jesus Christ, as the Son of God, could not be "holden of death". There were several variations of this general view. It is no longer widely held, although the word 'ransom' (cf. Matt. 20: 28) remains in the language of devotion, and the conception of Christ as victor over all the powers of evil is rightly retained.

Another type of theory is illustrated in the writings of Athanasius (about 296–373). It is sometimes called the mystical theory of atonement. By sinning, man had lost his original likeness to God (see 'Imago Dei'), and was therefore under condemnation of

2

death. When human nature was joined with the divine nature in the Incarnation of the Word, or Logos, of God, the image of God was restored to humanity: God became man, as Athanasius put it, in order that man might become divine. The death and resurrection of the God-man was the overcoming of death, and all who are incorporated in him have life eternal.

Anselm (about 1033–1109) denied that the Devil had any rights at all in man, and so repudiated the theory of ransom. Instead he regarded Jesus Christ in his passion and death as satisfying and, being the God-man, alone able to satisfy, the honour or dignity of God, which had been offended by man in sinning.

For Abelard (1079–1142), Christ's atoning work was directed not so much towards God, although God was party to and well-pleased with it, as towards man. It was the utmost pledge of God's love towards man even while a sinner (cf. John 3: 16; 1 John 4: 9–10), and as such it is the effectual means whereby men are moved to love God.

A markedly different theory, emphasizing especially some aspects of Pauline teaching, had often appeared in earlier writers, but was set forth with new power by the Protestant Reformers of the sixteenth and seventeenth centuries. It is usually known as the theory of penal substitution. Because of his sinfulness man has broken, and continues to break, those just laws of God which are expressions of his nature as righteous. All men therefore are under condemnation, and deserving of eternal punishment. In their stead Jesus Christ, the sinless Son of God incarnate, by his sacrificial death, bore the punishment due to men. All who put their faith in him, and are joined to him, are freed from condemnation and restored to fellowship with God (cf. Rom. 3: 9–26).

The jurist Grotius (1583–1645) put forward the view that the sin of man offended the fundamental, just principles on which the whole universe was founded by God. It could not possibly be overlooked. Christ's death, however, exhibited in the most exemplary way, as only the death of the very Son of God could do, that the sovereign rule of law must be upheld, and offences against it punished. Until such adequate satisfaction had been

3

made, reconciliation between God and sinners was impossible.

More recent theories tend to re-state either the theory of penal substitution, or some form of the moral (Abelardian) theory of atonement. It is no longer defensible to distinguish these two types as 'objective' and 'subjective'. Both terms can be applied to each of them. The first, however, is based on the conviction that God needs to be reconciled to man, as well as man to God. The other holds that it is man who needs to be reconciled to God; God's attitude to sinful men, and his dealings with them, are, and have always been, expressions of his righteous love. Another difference is apt to appear. The first type tends to concentrate attention upon the passion and death of Christ. The second holds that the teaching, healing ministry, and manner of life of Jesus Christ are more than a prelude to his death. With it, they form an integral part of his work as Saviour. (See also 'Reconciliation', 'Salvation'.)

ATTRIBUTES OF GOD are terms intended to express aspects of God's essential nature. Taken one by one they are partial, but complementary, answers to the question, What is meant by 'God'? Taken together, they should provide in out-line as complete an answer as in the nature of the case is possible.

The essential nature of God is knowable only in so far as God reveals himself. For theology, the primary written testimony to God's self-communication is found in Scripture, and above all in its witness to the revelation of God in and through Jesus Christ. When expounding the attributes of God, however, theologians have not confined themselves to Biblical language. Nor could they do so, if they were to interpret the faith of the Church to men of their own day. How far the terms they have used distort the witness of Scripture is constantly being discussed.

Various lists of divine attributes have been proposed. At the beginning of any detailed discussion of the attributes, however, it is important to emphasize the unity of God. That is implied by

4

the fact that 'God' is primarily a proper name (see 'God'). Each attribute, therefore, must be expounded in ways that harmonize with what is said about the other attributes. For questions which arise from this emphasis on the unity of God, see also the articles on 'Trinity', 'Christology', 'Atonement', and 'Holy Spirit'.

The attributes of God may conveniently be grouped into those which pertain to his sovereignty, and those which pertain to his love. Attributes relating to divine love include grace, holiness, mercy, righteousness, patience, and wisdom. These, and other terms of attribution, are Biblical words. In every age they call for fresh interpretation.

Attributes relating to divine sovereignty are often expressed in such terms as omnipotence, omniscience, omnipresence, and eternity. These words are meant to reflect Biblical witness to the nature of God, but because of their use in other ways they often give rise to misunderstanding. Omnipotence signifies the unqualified ability of God to employ every means to realize his purposes. The term has sometimes foolishly been taken to mean 'able to do anything'; in that sense, it raises many unnecessary conundrums. Even in its proper meaning, it gives rise to serious problems (see 'Providence'). Omniscience indicates the unqualified intelligence of God, the completeness of divine knowing, which includes foreseeing. In this connection, theologians discuss how far God can be said to foresee, without compromising the degree of freedom, however limited, which must be ascribed to a genuine person (see 'Person'). Omnipresence refers to God's superiority over the limitations of space, and signifies that God is active at every point in the universe. Eternity refers to divine superiority over the limitations of time, and signifies especially the changelessness of the character and purposes of God (see 'Eternity').

BELIEF is used in more than one way. It may refer to a state of mind, believing, which is more than sheer ignorance, but less than complete knowledge. For example, belief in the existence of God signifies a state of mind different from not knowing that God exists, and different also from knowing without any possibility of doubt whatsoever. Believing signifies a conviction so strong that the believer feels, thinks, and behaves as if it were true that God exists. In technical terms, such conviction is described as a high degree of certitude, as distinct from certainty. It should be noted, however, that in the Bible 'knowing' is often used for 'believing' in the sense just described.

Belief is used also to indicate, not a state of mind, but what is believed. The existence of God is one such belief. This usage cannot be separated entirely from the other, but failure to recognize the distinction between them often leads to confusion. For example, belief in the first sense can be investigated by students of psychology. The truth or otherwise of beliefs in the second sense, however, cannot be settled by examining mental processes, although some psychologists have taken upon themselves to do so.

(1) The psychology of religion includes a scientific description of belief in the first sense, i.e. believing, and analyses its causes. Some causes of belief are due to environment: for instance, the influence of parents, education, social traditions. Some causes are relatively private to each individual, such as his wishful thinking. Some causes of his believing may be known to a person; of others he is quite unaware. The varied causes of belief are intimately intermingled. For example, a person's believing that God exists may, to some extent, be due to admiration for someone who already believes in the existence of God. That other person is part of his environment. His admiration, however, is a reaction of his own. His own admiration is due to factors which are partly known to him, but partly quite unconscious. It is the business of psychology of religion to describe and analyse, not only believing, but also such related matters as disbelieving (definite dissenting) and doubting (the withholding of full assent, or keeping assent in suspense).

(2) The philosophy of religion, on the other hand, is concerned with a critical examination of belief in the second sense, namely,

6

what it is which is believed. It is concerned, not with the causes, but with the truth of beliefs.

(3) Theology has to do with belief in both senses of the term. The nature and causes of believing are important in the field of Practical Theology (for what this includes, see 'Theology'). The psychological study of believing makes contributions also to exegesis and interpretation of the Bible. It throws light on some aspects of Church history, including doctrinal controversy. It enters also into present-day discussions of the validity of faith.

Theology is much more concerned, however, with beliefs in the sense of past and present statements in which Christian faith, and its implications for thought and conduct, are expressed. Part of its task is to criticize the language of such statements, and to make them as clear and meaningful today as possible. Theology has also the task of exhibiting the truth of beliefs. Because faith is experience of God, it cannot be set out in beliefs which logically compel assent. Nevertheless, theology attempts to establish their truth along two lines. First, by showing their adequacy, above that of alternative statements, to express Christian experience; and second, by showing that they harmonize with one another, as well as fit in with other well-founded beliefs about the world and man. Because of the nature of faith, the beliefs which express it are bound to be in part "above reason", but theology proceeds on the assumption that true beliefs are nevertheless "according to reason". (See also 'Theology', 'Philosophy of Religion', 'Epistemology', 'Faith', 'Paradox'.)

CHRISTOLOGY is the doctrine of the person and the work of Christ. Sometimes the term is restricted to study of the person of Christ, and in particular the way in which he is both human and divine. His person, however, cannot be divorced from his saving work: faith in him begins with adoring recognition of him as both Lord and also Saviour.

For the orderly study of the work of Christ, a suggestion made

7

by Eusebius (about 260–340), referred to by Thomas Aquinas (about 1225–74), but fully developed by Calvin (1509–64), has proved fruitful. Christ, or the Messiah, means 'the anointed'. Eusebius pointed out that, in the Bible, three kinds of person are anointed to their office: prophets, priests, and kings. To avoid the dangers of discussing the prophetic, priestly, and royal offices of Christ separately, it is important to emphasize the unity of Christ's work: it is all for man's salvation.

Christ's prophetic work is what he did in speaking out, on God's behalf, to men concerning the past, the present, and the future. Such speaking out, like that of the Old Testament prophets, was not merely verbal. It included also his actions, his manner of life, and especially his passion and death. Jesus Christ exhibited compassion, forgave sinners, exposed and condemned sinfulness, taught the way of living as children of God. In doing this, he declared the mind of God, and evoked in his followers faith in God as both holy and loving.

Christ's priestly work is what he did on behalf of men, especially so far as their standing and relationships with God the Father are concerned. According to New Testament witness, there is nothing in the relationship between the Father and the Son but complete oneness in loving and righteous purpose. Christ does not wring benefits for mankind from a reluctant deity. Christ's priestly work is the gift of God (cf. John 3: 16; 2 Cor. 5: 19. See also 'Atonement').

What the New Testament says, or implies, about the kingly work of Christ cannot be separated from recognition of him as a royal person. The symbolic language used of Christ, as set down on the right hand of God, or seated on his throne, refers to both. His kingly work is particularly associated with his headship over the Church. What Christ did on earth in the days of his humiliation, he is bringing, and will bring, to completion, now that he is risen from the dead and lives for evermore (see 'Eschatology'). This kingly work is being accomplished through the Holy Spirit. (See also 'Holy Spirit', 'Salvation'.)

All this is clearly bound up with doctrine concerning the

person of Christ. The doctrine is rooted in historical witness to what he said, and did, and revealed himself to be, in the days of his flesh. It stems also from the witness of the disciples ever since to the continuing activity of their living Master. The doctrine is a sustained attempt to answer the question (Mark 8: 29), 'Who do you say that I am?'

That Jesus was like other men, that he was genuinely human, is part of the Biblical testimony. So also is the recognition that Jesus was different from all other men. He was so different in what he said and did, and he is so different in what he is and does in the experience of the Christian community, that to speak of him as human is completely inadequate. The New Testament writers did not favour the word divine, no doubt because of its pagan associations. They did speak of Jesus as Lord. This title challenged both Jews and Gentiles, because it was used also of God.

Beginning with the conviction that Jesus is both human and also rightly entitled Lord, theology has to wrestle with questions that fall into two main groups. First, in what ways can Christians most adequately express the relationship between what in Jesus is human and what in him is divine? Second, in what ways can Christians express most adequately the relationship between him, who is both human and divine, and God? In every generation not the least part of the theological task is to determine in what sort of terms these questions ought to be framed. (See also 'Trinity', 'Substance'.)

COSMOLOGICAL ARGUMENTS begin with matters of fact about the world ('cosmos') and from them attempt to demonstrate the existence of God. For example, some things in the world are in motion. This would not be so, unless they were moved by something else. That something else, in turn, is moved by yet another, and so on. We cannot rest, however, in the thought of an endless series (what is technically called an 'infinite regress') of causes of motion. There must be an un-moved first mover. That is what is called God.

Although this argument raises questions as to what 'motion' is, and other difficulties, the chief objection is apt to be: Why stop the series at a first mover at all? No answer is forthcoming, so long as the argument is concerned with a series of movers within the natural order. The argument by itself breaks down; but it is useful in suggesting that, beyond the series of natural things, there is need to account for the series itself. That cannot be done, the argument suggests, apart from conceiving a reality other than the whole series, i.e. a transcendental reality (see 'Immanence and Transcendence').

Another form of the argument starts from the observation that one thing is produced, or caused, by another. The reasoning proceeds, as in the other case, to a first cause, which is called God. The meaning of 'cause' and 'causation' has been much debated. Apart from that, similar objections and comments apply to this as to the other form of the argument. So it is with the argument which states that we cannot be content to observe that things just happen to be in existence. We must, it is said, conclude that there is some reality which necessarily exists, reality which does not depend for its existence on anything else (see 'Ontological Arguments'), and this is God.

A fourth form of the argument begins with the fact that we judge some things in the world to be more or less good, more or less noble, even more or less real, and more or less true. To speak in this way, however, reveals the further fact that we are making use of a standard by which to judge them, or rather by which they are judged. There must be then a best, a completely real, and something altogether perfect. This we call God.

Such arguments put forward by Thomas Aquinas (about 1225–74), Descartes (1596–1650), and Locke (1632–1704) were criti-cized, along lines already mentioned, by Hume (1711–76) and Kant (1724–1804). The debate goes on. Apart from the view that the universe must just be accepted as unintelligible brute fact, the arguments continue to suggest that the world as we know it calls for some explanation, which cannot be found within it. As such, they still have a part to play in the dialogue between those who believe in the God and Father of Jesus Christ and those who are enquiring about the validity of religious experience and the truth of Christian beliefs (see 'Philosophy of Religion').

COSMOLOGY is ordered discourse about the nature of the universe, regarded as a whole that has been formed according to a pattern or plan. Such studies have often been taken to include discussion of how the universe came into existence; but for that discussion it is better to use another term, cosmogony. In the past, philosophy and natural science have been much concerned with both the origins and pattern of the universe. In recent times, however, many philosophers have turned away from such questions, either because they regard the questions as 'limit' problems inaccessible to investigation or because their interests have shifted. The systematic theologian, on the other hand, even while acknowledging the inescapable limitations of human knowledge in this field, cannot put the subject aside.

With regard to the beginnings of the universe, a theology which is Biblically based is bound to express the conviction (see 'Creation') that they are due to the sovereign will of God and his purposes, and is bound to deal with the problems which such conviction entails. Moreover, with regard to the pattern, or ways of working, of the universe as a whole, as well as of the earth as part of it, theology is bound to express the conviction that it is designed by and remains within the control of God. This too raises questions with which theologians are perpetually occupied (see, e.g. 'Providence').

A long-standing question is the significance for faith, and consequently for theology, of the actual Biblical statements about the beginnings and structure of the physical universe. Few theologians would take such statements today as scientific statements, or attempt to justify them as such by reinterpreting terms within them – such as regarding the 'days' of creation as unspecified periods of time, which however succeeded one another in the order stated in the Bible. Another concern of the theologian is to consider the challenge to Christian thought of deductions from scientific investigation which appear to discredit essential Christian convictions. Just to mention a classical example, the innumerable galaxies of uninhabited heavenly bodies, and their vast extent, have often been taken as making quite incredible Christian faith in the compassionate care of the Creator for so infinitesimally small a portion of the astral universe as the earth, let alone for each human being. Theology remains open to the light thrown by science upon the nature and pattern of the physical universe, and the human situation within it. Theology is not irrevocably committed, however, to any particular scientific theory. In its task of expressing Christian doctrine for the present age, it is bound to make illustrative use of current scientific views. It must do so, nevertheless, in full view of two lessons from the past: all scientific views on such large matters are subject to drastic changes, and theology has already suffered much from a too uncritical adherence to scientific hypotheses which appeared to hold the field. (See also 'Myth', 'Theology'.)

COVENANT is a key Biblical word, but its use in theology has varied. The notion of covenant was made the basis of a specific type of theology (covenantal, or federal, theology). As a system it has mostly been abandoned, but the notion of covenant is still influential.

The Old Testament use of the term is generally, though not always, controlled by recognition of the fact that God's dealings with individuals (e.g. Noah, Abraham) and their families, and with Israel as an elect people, are due to the graciousness of God (see 'Grace'). Covenant is, therefore, not to be understood as a pact entered into by two parties for their mutual benefit. It is entirely God's gift. Under the covenant, God guides his people, raises up leaders for them, and reveals his will. God is ever faithful to the covenant. But it can be broken. As a personal relationship, it can be broken by the sinfulness of God's people.

The New Testament use of covenant is controlled by the same recognition of God's unwearied, gracious attitude and activity. On the testimony of Old Testament prophets, God's covenant with Israel had been broken. A new covenant had been promised. And one way of proclaiming the Gospel was to affirm that God, in his steadfast love, had given Jesus Christ to fulfil that promise.

Various covenants are mentioned in the Bible. Following a line of thought suggested by Paul (see 1 Cor. 15), covenantal or federal theology based itself on the view that God covenanted first with Adam, as the representative of all human kind. This covenant required Adam's complete obedience to God's commands, and promised in return deathless life. When Adam failed to keep the covenant, mankind was deprived of life eternal. Nevertheless, by the mercy of God, that old covenant, the 'covenant of works' as it was called, was replaced by the 'covenant of grace'. The new covenant was made by God with Jesus Christ as the second Adam. He was perfectly obedient to God, even unto the cross. Therefore, to those who are united to Christ by faith, God grants both forgiveness and eternal life.

This type of Reformed Theology, arising towards the end of the sixteenth century, influential in the seventeenth and eighteenth centuries, and worked out with elaborate care, has largely succumbed to the criticism of inconsistency in its doctrine of God. It suggested that, under the old covenant at any rate, God rewarded men according to their merits. This would imply a change of mind and attitude in God, if it was to be made consistent with the renewed insight of the Reformers into the Gospel. For the Gospel, as embodied in Jesus Christ, proclaims the utter graciousness of God towards penitent sinners (see 'Justification by Faith').

In more recent theology, the 'new covenant' in Christ is used to express the graciousness of God in electing a new chosen people. The new covenant is with the Church but, like the old Israel, the new people of God are elected, not only to be blessed themselves, but also to be God's agents in fulfilling his eternal purposes for mankind. Indeed the new covenant, under which the Church of Christ was formed and is sustained, is linked organically with the old covenant, under which Israel was formed and sustained. This use of the term covenant provides a key to a Christian interpretation of human history, as the fulfilling of God's purpose in creation and redemption, a purpose which is to be consummated in the 'last days'. (See also 'Election', 'Providence', 'Creation', 'Eschatology'.)

CREATION, as theological doctrine, expounds an affirmation of faith (cf. Heb. 11: 3), and in the nature of the case cannot be a matter of historical evidence. The affirmations and denials implied in the doctrine are to be tested by their coherence within a total statement of Christian beliefs.

Those affirmations and denials are implicit in the paradoxical phrase, 'creation out of nothing' (see 2 Macc. 7: 28, and cf. Rom. 4: 17, Heb. 11: 3). The doctrine denies that God is identifiable with all that is (pantheism). It also denies that 'matter', or the natural order, including man, exists or ever existed independently of God's creative work (see 'Teleological Arguments'). In positive terms, it affirms God's otherness from the natural order, however much the otherness of God must be qualified in terms of his intimacy with it (see 'Immanence and Transcendence'). It also affirms that the natural order owes its being to God; in its entirety, it belongs to him.

From all this, three things follow which the doctrine goes on to make clear. First, the natural order can never rightly claim man's supreme allegiance. Nature-worship is idolatry. Second, the natural order is not to be despised, nor is it evil. Some attitudes of mind towards things physical, and some forms of asceticism, offend against the insights of faith which the doctrine of creation

14

affirms. The order of nature, despite the difficulties for faith of interpreting some of its features (see 'Providence'), shows forth the glory of God, and is a sphere in which God is working out his purposes (see Rom. 11: 36; 8: 38–39; Col. 1: 16). Third, the natural order has been given a relative independence of God. It is not like a watch which has been wound up and, with occasional adjustments, left to go on its own. Nevertheless, it has been planted out by the Creator as a living universe, and not a mere puppet show.

The creation of human kind, as part of the doctrine of creation, emphasizes man's utter dependence upon God for his being (see 'Ontology'). This also has consequences, which the doctrine sets out. First, no man or group of men, or humanity as a whole, can rightly claim anyone's unconditional allegiance. Such worship would also be idolatry. Second, no man ought to be despised, for as a man he is a creature of God. Third, man as God's creation is made for God's sovereign, gracious purposes (see 'Imago Dei'). Man's destiny is indissolubly bound up with God's will. But, fourth, man also has been given a relative independence – in his case, we can speak of it as freedom – in relation to God, on whom he utterly depends (see 'Grace'). This relative independence can be expressed in terms of human responsibility; that is to say, man's ability to respond to God, and his accountability to God for the way in which he does respond.

ELECTION is a term which gives rise to confusion, for it has been used theologically in a variety of ways. For one thing, it is apt to be used interchangeably with 'predestination', a term better reserved for use in connection with the final consummation of God's purposes with men (see 'Predestination'). Five points may be set out in unfolding the Biblical use of 'election' and cognate expressions, and therefore the significance of the word for theology.

First, election conveys an essential part of Biblical testimony to the self-disclosed character of God. In fulfilling his purposes with mankind God exercises what, by analogy with human experience, can only be called choice. The term summarizes, therefore, part of the Biblical witness to the living God as personal.

Second, although God's purposes involve other kinds of choices, the use of this particular term emphasizes and is related to God's choice of persons in effecting human salvation.

Third, election is not confined to the choice of persons for their own blessedness. In the guiding and discipline of Israel, for example, God's election is exercised in the calling of agents or instruments of his purpose who are themselves ignorant, or even enemies, of God.

Fourth, from Biblical testimony as a whole it is plain that divine election for blessedness is not unrelated to the trustful, obedient response of those whom God has so elected. For example, the whole people of Israel is elected for blessedness. Unfaithfulness on the part of many, however, leads to their subsequent rejection by God. It is the faithful remnant who then become the elect. St Paul's complicated argument as a whole in *Romans* does not deny this, although it includes also the fervent hope that in the end all Israel will be saved. Similar statements apply to the use of 'elect' in connection with the whole Church of Christ and particular congregations.

Closely connected with this point, election to blessedness is characteristically related in the Bible to election to responsibility under God. Those who are blessed are called to be a blessing. This recurrent note in the prophetic tradition of Israel is clearly sounded also in the New Testament – not least in our Lord's criticism of Pharisees and lawyers (cf. Luke 11: 52). The distinctively Christian doctrine of election, indeed, is reflected in the description of Jesus Christ as both Lord and servant (cf. Phil. 2: 6–11). And his Church, the new Israel, the elect of God, like the old Israel, is called to be both a redeemed and a redeeming community (e.g. cf. Isa. 2: 2–3; 49: 6; 1 Pet. 1: 1; 2: 9).

EMPIRICAL ARGUMENTS for the existence of God are based on human experience. Experience, however, is a word with more than one meaning, and therefore the source of much confusion, both in theology and in philosophy. It may stand for experiencing; or, for what is experienced. While the Cosmological and Teleological Arguments for the existence of God rely more upon what is experienced by man, the Empirical Arguments begin rather from man's experiencing.

The first empirical argument states that humans are essentially 'religious'; in Calvin's language, there is in every man a seed of religion. The developed expression of this universal experience is belief in one God. Therefore, the existence of God is at least highly probable. This argument is often called the argument from general consent. In reply, it will be said that there is no general agreement among men as to belief in one supreme spiritual being. Even if there were, we should have to reckon with the possibility of universally mistaken beliefs: at one time, for example, it was universally believed that the earth was flat. All that the argument can show is this: if the belief is justifiable on other grounds, then the facts which the argument from general consent relies upon would reinforce belief in God's existence.

The same sort of comment would be made on the second argument. This is based on every man's desire for happiness, or good. It goes on to argue, first, that a desire so universal surely tells us something about the kind of universe in which man lives; second, that the world of nature and of human relationships is found to be incapable of fully satisfying this in-built desire; third, it can be satisfied only if God, who is sovereign goodness, exists.

The third argument is called the Pragmatic Argument. It seeks to deduce the existence of God from the beneficial effects in practical life which follow from holding such a belief. There is no doubt that belief in God has had profound and wide effects for good. But, it will be said, the belief has also had bad effects. It has multiplied the fears of many, it has increased a crippling sense of guilt, it has led some people to a kind of fatalism, and it has been responsible for intolerance towards unbelievers, even to the

17

extent of cruel torture and the waging of war. If true beliefs often have, for a time at least, distressing effects, and if false beliefs sometimes have beneficial results, most of the weight of the argument is surely lost.

The fourth type of empirical argument relies upon consciousness of personal encounter with God. Many people are convinced that in religious experience they have direct contact with God. Therefore, God undoubtedly exists. This argument from 'immediate' awareness of God takes two forms. It may be based on experience which is open only to a few, and is called mysticism proper (see 'Mysticism'). It may be based, however, on religious experience which is open to all, and is sometimes called 'heart religion'.

This is the most important of the empirical arguments. As an argument which is meant to convince those who do not have religious experience, or rather do not recognize any part of their experience as 'religious', it is defective. The reason is that faith (see 'Faith'), in the sense of awareness of being confronted by God, is intimately bound up with beliefs; and it is the truth of the latter which the argument is unable to show. After all, it will be said, the presence of a non-physical reality is a well-known delusion of the insane. Whether any experience of the kind which is used in the argument is to be judged valid or not, depends upon considerations other than the mere experience itself. Otherwise we should not be able to distinguish between the obsessions of the mentally abnormal and the convictions of other people. Indeed, we should not be able to distinguish between some of our vivid dreams and the experience of everyday life (see 'Philosophy of Religion'). By itself, the argument as an argument is not convincing. The facts upon which it is based, however, along with other considerations, may rightly be brought into any dialogue between believers and unbelievers which is seeking to remove intellectual barriers to faith.

EPISTEMOLOGY, or theory of knowledge, is of great importance for theology. The ways in which man can know anything, and the nature and the tests of truth, go to the roots
of Christian encounter with the most serious non-Christian
views (see 'Theology'). They also bear on divergent Christian
convictions concerning such central themes as revelation and
faith.

The problem about knowing is this. It is at one and the same
time an activity of each individual person, and yet a claim to be
the perceiving and understanding of reality which is other than
himself. How can that claim be justified? How can anyone ever
be sure that he knows anything other than his own opinions, or
the collective opinions of other people? Everyone lives on the
assumption that the physical world and other persons can be
known by himself, and everyone tests the assumption by acting
as if it were true. It is impossible to solve the problem in theory,
however, except by making another assumption. This is that
whatever can be known is active in making itself knowable to us.
This assumption can also be verified. It is verified by the fact that
the more anyone is alert and diligent in trying to perceive and
understand the world in which he lives, the more it makes itself
known to him. New or growing knowledge must then be tested,
in the same ways as knowledge we already have. Does it fit in
with what we already know, or think we know? Does the
experience of living in our environment, and dealing with it,
confirm such new knowledge, or not?

The theory of knowledge discusses the difficulties raised by
what has just been said. It also examines the kind of language
used in such discussion. Epistemology is clearly relevant to
theology; for theology is based upon the conviction that God,
although transcendent (see 'Immanence and Transcendence'), is
knowable by man, and that God is continually making himself
known to men. (See also 'Revelation', 'Faith', 'God'.)

ESCHATOLOGY, or doctrine concerning the 'last things', has to do with the consummation of God's purposes in creation, and particularly in the making of man. The doctrine is rooted in Christian assurance of salvation. Salvation relates to the past, because God accepts men as sinners, and shares with them in dealing with the consequences of past disobedience. (See also 'Sin', 'Atonement', 'Justification by Faith'.) Salvation relates to the present, because by faith men live now as members of God's household, supported and guided by the Holy Spirit. (See also 'Faith', 'Sanctification', 'Holy Spirit'.) But salvation relates also to the future, because it includes a conviction of the sovereignty of God over all creation, and over all the affairs of men (see 'Providence').

The Biblical basis for teaching about the future compels us to distinguish between what it is essential to affirm about Christian hope, and the kind of imagery in which such hope has been expressed (see 'Myth'). Before the coming of Jesus, Jewish confidence that God would vindicate his people had expressed itself in terms of violent upheavals in the natural world, and terrible disasters among men, as signs of the coming of the Messiah. Moreover, there would be wars between angelic hosts and satanic powers. There was to be a rule of the righteous ones, for a time, on the earth. The dead would be raised. A final assize, the punishment of the wicked, and a new creation, all featured in the expression of confidence that God would intervene to overthrow the might of entrenched wrongdoing, and make a fresh start for those who belonged to him. Jesus himself made use of some of this imagery, and his followers even more. To dismiss such forms of expression as mere historical curiosities, is not to take the Incarnation seriously. It is taking it seriously, however, to regard them as symbols, rather than as literal truths, and to try in each generation to set forth what it is to which, through them, Jesus testified. His testimony can only be made plain if we take into account the teaching of Jesus as a whole, and the events of his life, passion, resurrection, and ascension.

The Christian doctrine of the last things includes convictions concerning the resurrection of the dead, the second coming of Christ, the final judgement, and the new heaven and new earth. Teaching on the resurrection of the dead is not based on some theory of the immortality of the soul, imprisoned for a time in a physical, corruptible body. It rests on Christian doctrine concerning God's purpose for each person (see 'Imago Dei'), and in the assurance, grounded in Christ's resurrection, that those who put their trust in him shall not perish. For further questions which arise in this connection, see 'Predestination' and 'Universalism'. The 'second coming' of Christ has been interpreted in several ways in the course of the history of doctrine, but essentially it is the statement that God's sovereign purpose, which prepared the way for the Incarnation, and was most fully revealed in the days of his flesh, will be completed. The final judgement, expressed as we said, in terms of a final assize, with the dispensation of rewards (heaven) and punishments (hell), is a vivid way of expressing, with the utmost seriousness, the consequences of obedience and disobedience to God (see 'Sin'). Distinctively Christian teaching on this matter must be controlled throughout by the evangelical assurance, that God's attitude to sinners beyond the grave is all of a piece with his attitude towards sinners in this life, as that is manifested in the life, teaching, and passion of Christ. Teaching on the new heaven and the new earth is a way of stating Christian convictions that the divine purpose, expressed in the doctrine of creation, will be carried through to completion.

The modern term 'realized eschatology' summarizes the view that, with the coming of Jesus Christ, the kingdom of God is here and now a present reality among men. References in the Scriptures to the future, it is said, may be dismissed by Christians today as just the ephemeral beliefs of the early Church. This view hardly expresses fully what Christian doctrine concerning the last things needs to affirm. The kingdom of God, opened by Christ to all believers, is certainly a present reality, but the doctrine takes seriously, and tries to reinterpret, those beliefs about the future which are grounded in teaching about Christ's coming and work. (See also 'Christology', 'Eternity'.)

ETERNITY is used in theology in several ways. On the one hand, it signifies unending time, or duration. This usage corresponds to the most general Biblical ways of thinking and speaking. It is indeed the way in which the term is most generally employed in everyday speech by ourselves. On reflection, however, the notion of unending time gives rise to problems which have puzzled philosophers and theologians. What chiefly concerns theology, however, as the expression of Christian faith is this: to apply any notion of temporal succession to God, even temporal succession without beginning or end, appears to detract from God's sovereignty and perfection. For example, time might then appear to be primordial to God, and God in some way to be himself subject to time. Again, all successiveness in time implies that what is past is irrevocable; therefore, on this view of eternity, there must be an element of loss in the very life of God. Faced with such difficulties, most theologians regard the attribution of eternity to God, in the sense of endless duration, as at best a useful, and perhaps necessary, metaphor based upon human experience of temporal succession.

Because the metaphor seems to imply what Christian reflection upon the self-disclosure of God is bound to deny, the term eternity has also been used theologically in the sense of timeless perfection. So used it carries more than the sense of complete goodness. It signifies that of the being or life of God no conceivable lack may be predicated: nothing needs to be added to God or taken away. The influence of Greek ways of thought upon theology is apparent in this move from the moral to the metaphysical use of the word perfection.

Closely linked with the use of eternity in the sense of timeless perfection is its use to signify immutability. In the context of Biblical thought, the unchanging and unchangeable nature of God is expressed in terms of his steadfastness in purpose and attitude towards mankind. In later theology, however, the expression of Biblical testimony became cross-fertilized by classical Greek thought, for which the working out of purposes, and the successiveness that involves, was incompatible with changelessness. It is Aristotle's conception of eternity as change-less activity which, for example, is echoed in Thomas Aquinas's characterization of God as pure act.

EXISTENTIALISM is a manner of philosophizing from the standpoint of one who is involved, as a complex human being, in the community of his fellows, and in the world in which he finds himself. It is opposed to philosophizing from the standpoint of one who tries to be "a spectator of all time and all existence" (Plato). Existentialists fiercely criticize the tradition which regards man's reasoning powers as excellent above all other aspects of his nature. For example, Kierkegaard (1813–55), the father of modern existentialism, wrote of the rationalist philosopher Hegel (1770–1831), that he had absent-mindedly forgotten "what it means to be a human being". Instead of asking abstract questions like, "What is man?", the existentialist prefers to ask, "Who am I?", and "What is the situation, here and now, in which I find myself?" For him, traditional abstract terms, like 'substance' and 'soul', throw no light whatever on the mystery of the human self. They only obscure it. No reasoning can penetrate the mysteriousness of each one's lived experience. The existentialist does not despise the intellect. When expressing himself in philosophical works, he does not abandon the use of careful, critical, and abstract language – far from it. Nevertheless, the essential mystery of each human being, and of his actual situation, is exhibited better through novels, drama, films, and poetry. Such media enable us to become involved in the situations set out by the author, as distinct from merely looking at them from the outside. Some existentialists, therefore, in addition to producing books of philosophy, have used these literary and visual media with great effect.

The existentialism of recent times reflects the pessimism, and the sense of revulsion, which many have felt as a result of the cruelties of modern war, as well as the oppressions, confusion, and hardships caused by social revolutionary movements. To existentialists, the traditional teaching of moralists, philosophers, and religious bodies, reveals an uncomprehending indifference, on the part of privileged and conventional persons, to the realities of the human situation.

The great variety of forms of existentialism, atheist and Christian, cannot be described here. It must be said, however, that the movement as a whole has profoundly influenced modern theology. This shows itself in renewed criticism of the influence of rationalism in theology; in fresh emphasis on the fact and mystery of confrontation between God and man, with its implications for the understanding of the nature of faith; and in the prominence given to such themes as 'decision' and 'commitment'.

FAITH is used in several ways. In its principal sense, it signifies personal recognition of the presence of the living God, and response to him in trust and obedience. It is thus correlative to revelation, as the self-communication of God. In the Bible, and in theological writing, faith is often used in the sense of trust, or confidence, in God – 'fiducia' is the technical term. Of course, this presupposes acknowledgement of the being and presence of God, but it lays most stress on the feeling aspect of faith. Sometimes faith is used with emphasis on its volitional aspect, and then indicates venture, or active commitment. Sometimes faith carries a chiefly intellectual meaning. In that case, it signifies a total interpretation of the universe and mankind in terms of the being and purposes of God, the emotional and volitional factors in faith falling rather into the background. Perhaps it is worth adding, that faith, as used in theology at any rate, is not an equivalent to credulity, or illogical belief in the improbable.

Used in its principal sense, faith must be distinguished from beliefs (see 'Belief', and also the next paragraph). It should also be marked off from such terms as 'the Faith', or 'a faith', or 'faiths': all these usually refer to an organized body of beliefs, or

24

doctrines. Faith is also used in a special sense (especially by Eastern Orthodox and Roman Catholic writers) when it signifies assent to doctrines promulgated on the unquestionable authority of the Church.

While faith, in its principal sense, should be distinguished from beliefs, the two are intimately conjoined. As recognition or acknowledgement of the living God, faith always presupposes beliefs of some sort, however undeveloped, about divine reality. Second, faith as experience of God may at any stage enlarge, or otherwise modify, antecedent beliefs. This is clearly seen in the development of Old Testament thought about God, and also (see 'Christology') in the New Testament. Third, antecedent beliefs can have the effect of restricting the present range of a person's experience of God. The 'righteousness' of some Pharisees, for example, prevented them from being open to God's forgiving love of a penitent, sinful woman, and some interpretations of the 'wrath of God' have had a similar effect on some Christians.

The intermingling of faith and beliefs introduces another matter: the great importance of religious communities for the life and thought of individual believers; and of the variety of religious communities for the life and thought of each community. The faith and beliefs of any individual believer presuppose the faith and beliefs of other people, but often need, at any stage, to be corrected by those of the religious community to which he belongs. On the other hand, as in the case of Old Testament prophets, or Peter, Paul, and Luther, for example, an individual's experience of God may greatly enlarge, and correct, the faith and beliefs of the religious community. But that is not all. A community as a whole may be governed by beliefs which restrict the range and quality of the religious experience of all its members. To outsiders this is apparent in the case of some sects, or other groups of Christians; but it is, in some measure, true of every religious community. This has been brought home to many who have been involved in the ecumenical movement. To correct partiality, each Christian community needs to be confronted with the faith and beliefs of others.

C

A further point concerns the 'paradox of faith'. Faith is both a gift and a task. It is the gift of God; for it is awakened, directly or indirectly, through the continuous gracious initiative of God, who makes himself known in manifold ways to individuals and communities. Faith is also a human responsibility. It involves each man's recognition and response to the self-disclosure of God. Man is a responsible being, in the double sense of 'able to respond' to the approach of the living God, but also 'accountable' for the kind of response he makes. (See also 'Belief', 'Grace', 'Revelation', 'Justification by Faith', 'Theology'.)

GOD is in the language of devotion a proper name. In theology it is also used as a descriptive term. The Christian doctrine of God is, in large measure, an attempt to make plain what is intended by the use of this term; to vindicate its significance against objections; and to draw out its implications for thought and conduct.

Distinctively Christian faith (see 'Faith') arises from confrontation with "the God and Father of our Lord Jesus Christ", but Christian faith is historically continuous with Jewish faith in God. God was, and is, supremely and decisively manifested in Jesus Christ; but God manifest in Jesus Christ is God already manifested, less clearly, in and through Israel (cf. Heb. 1: 1-4). For the earliest Christians, therefore, God as a descriptive term (or, 'the idea of God' as it is sometimes, but not very happily, put) already had a rich significance. The history and development of Jewish beliefs, prior to the coming of Jesus, is beyond the scope of this article; but what the term had come to signify may be broadly stated as follows: The only God; the creator and governor of the universe, and of mankind; while transcendent over all, yet in personal relationships with man; righteous and steadfast in love to mankind, yet concerned with each individual; a self-disclosing God, who makes his character and will known in part through the natural order, and human history, but who has done so

26

clearly in the formation, discipline, and enlightenment of the people of Israel; merciful towards repentant sinners; desirous that men should exercise mercy and loving-kindness towards their fellows. Moreover, God has yet to manifest himself more fully in the future, and will do so, in carrying through to completion his sovereign purposes for the world and mankind.

As a descriptive term, God included all such beliefs, when it was used by the first Christians. Some Jewish beliefs were given fresh emphasis, or modified, in the teaching of Jesus. All of them, however, were transmuted, when the disciples came to recognize Jesus as having a unique relationship with God, describable by such terms as Messiah, or Christ, Lord, and Son of the living God (see 'Christology').

Jewish beliefs, meantime, were being expressed in new ways by Jews in contact with Gentile, and especially Greek, ways of thinking. As the Christian movement spread beyond Palestine, the expression of distinctively Christian beliefs, also, had to be adapted to Greek and Latin forms of thought. This was necessary, in order to clarify and build up the faith of Christians living amid non-Jewish cultures; and also to assist in the conversion of non-Christians. Some theologians have held that, in this process, the significance of God as a descriptive term was radically changed. Certainly, the way in which it has been used in much theological debate, and in some statements of faith, is alien to Biblical usage. Nevertheless, by the end of the fourth century, the primacy of the Scriptures had become more and more firmly established. In consequence, while Christian beliefs about God continued to be translated into terms of Latin and Greek thought, the Biblical terms remained as a constant challenge to them, even when the challenge was little heeded. The tension in theological discussion, then and now, is not so much over the need for re-stating Christian beliefs. It is rather between those who regard the terms of current thought as useful, in bringing out the fuller meaning of Biblical statements about God, and those who regard them as seriously distorting the significance of Biblical terms.

At present, this age-long tension has taken a rather different turn. Some theologians contend that all traditional language about God, Biblical as well as non-Biblical, is apt to be highly misleading. It is partly based on false analogies from human experience, and on out-moded beliefs about the universe. The linguistic analysis of theological statements is one of the major preoccupations of some theologians today. This is important in discussing God as a descriptive term. It is subordinate, however, to what is signified by the use of 'God' as a proper name. In other words, it is subordinate to awareness of, and personal confrontation with, the living God. Such awareness, without which theology tends to become a kind of word-game, continues to be awakened, to no small extent, by the use, in worship and preaching, of the language of the Bible. In stating the doctrine of God, therefore, the theological task must continue to include the work of reconciling the analogical language of Scripture with non-Scriptural language, in which modern knowledge and reflection are expressed. (See also 'Myth', 'Analogy', 'Symbol'.)

GRACE, which in everyday speech signifies elegance, charm, or favour, is used, in theology, primarily for the unmerited, active loving-kindness of God towards man. Other uses are based on this fundamental meaning. Grace is manifested and mediated, above all, in and through Jesus Christ as Saviour. Hence Paul can write of 'the grace of the Lord Jesus Christ'. Faith itself (see 'Faith') is awakened by grace. The doctrine of grace is basic, not only for the doctrine of salvation, but also for Christian teaching on creation, providence, and eschatology.

In worshipful acknowledgement of the grace of God, all the main Christian traditions are at one. Serious disagreements appear, however, in theological statements about grace. This is particularly plain in the ways in which the term is used when discussing those effects, or gifts, which are consequences of the grace of God.

For example, Eastern Orthodox and Roman Catholic Churches,

speaking broadly, tend to teach that, to be saved, man must be changed essentially from fallen human nature to divine nature. This requires a transfusion, or infusion, of supernatural power, and that power is called grace. By such transfusion, or infusion, a man acquires the supernatural virtues of faith, hope, and love. This saving grace is available to sinful men, because of the atoning death of Jesus Christ, who was both perfectly human and perfectly divine. However, it is normally available to penitents through the Church alone. It is channelled through the sacraments, which are 'means of grace' in this sense (see note on Transubstantiation in 'Substance'; 'Sacraments').

The 'catholic' doctrine does not deny man's natural powers of reason, or freedom of the will. A man can make, or refuse to make, submission to the claims of the Church to be a supernatural and unique organ of grace. He is responsible, moreover, for the exercise of the supernatural virtues he acquires. Indeed, the meritorious exercise of them is necessary for attaining to the ultimate blessedness of heaven, and the vision of God. Nevertheless, to speak of the infusion of grace seems, to other Christians, to be using 'grace' in a less than personal way; and the transaction itself sounds something like the transfer of a commodity. The drift of such teaching, however refined its fuller expression may be, is taken to have serious consequences, not only in doctrine, but also in practice.

Such criticism is characteristic of the Reformed or Protestant Church tradition. In that tradition, grace is a short way of expressing the unmeritable, but steadfast and active, love of God towards man. The Christian life begins with the personal response of a sinner to the proclaimed Gospel, repentance and glad acceptance of God's offer of forgiveness. It is marked throughout by personal response to the graciousness of God. (See also 'Justification by Faith', 'Sanctification'.) The gifts of grace, on this view, are not transferable endowments. They are the dynamic attitudes, and ways of living, which grow from such a personal relationship between the living God and man. The 'means of grace' are the manifold ways in which this relationship is nurtured

29

by God, and confirmed. They include the duties and opportunities of everyday life; but chief among them are the fellowship of the Church as the Body of Christ, and the ministry of the Word and sacraments within it.

HERMENEUTICS is the science of the principles of interpretation. It should be distinguished from exegesis, which is the application of such principles to a particular text. For theology, hermeneutics is of prime importance in connection with the Bible, but it is important also in connection with those other writings which bear upon the origin and development of Christian doctrine.

It is now generally agreed, that interpretation of a Biblical passage includes an attempt to find its exact meaning for the author himself. This was not always thought necessary. Other principles were preferred, and some still are. This is understandable. The plain, literal meaning of some statements in the Bible is puzzling, and in some cases is offensive to Christian thought and piety. To justify the place of such statements in Holy Scripture, it was thought necessary to apply the principle of allegorical interpretation. For example, by treating it as an allegory, the Song of Songs was interpreted as an inspired utterance of God's love for his people. The literal meaning is thus abandoned. Another principle is called typology. For example, the divine provision of food and drink for the Israelites, in their journeying through the wilderness, is taken as a type of the bread and wine divinely given in the sacrament of the Lord's Supper. This is not abandoning the literal meaning of the text, but finding in it an intended profounder meaning.

To find the exact meaning for the author himself of what he wrote is a comprehensive, and often a very difficult, task. It needs, first, a wide and detailed knowledge of the language in which it was written, and of affiliated languages. Again, the interpreter must make sure that what he is studying are the exact words of the original. This is sometimes far from easy. In the case of some mutilated passages, it is impossible. No book of the Bible is available in its original form. All we have are copies of copies, and in places the available copies differ from one another. Even that is not all. The interpreter has to understand, as far as possible, what the words and sentences would be taken to mean at the time they were written, as distinct from what they may have come later to mean. This involves study of the historical and cultural setting amid which the author did his work.

Biblical interpretation, then, includes a sustained attempt to find the plain and literal meaning of any passage in its historical setting. That however is not enough by itself. For the theologian, the Bible is testimony to the self-disclosure of the living God (see 'Holy Scripture'). The plain meaning of any particular part, therefore, takes on added significance from its relationship to the plain meaning, in their historical setting, of earlier and later passages. A further principle of interpretation then appears. Different parts of the Bible are to be interpreted, in part, as linked in the story of the self-communication of God, and of the apprehension by man of the nature and eternal purposes of God (see 'Word of God').

HOLY is applied, primarily, to God; second, to whatever is associated with, set apart for, or dedicated to the service of God; and, third, as 'the holy', to the distinctively emotional factor in apprehending the presence of God. For holy, or holiness, as applied to the Christian life, see 'Sanctification'.

As applied to God, holiness does not signify one attribute among others, but rather the otherness of God's being and perfection from all that is not God. To explain the meaning of 'holy', such words as separation and unapproachableness are often used. Uniqueness is perhaps a better term. God is not a divinity, but alone divine. God as holy indicates the transcendence of God (see 'Immanence and Transcendence').

31

As applied to special persons, documents, ordinances, buildings, furnishings and so on, associated with or set apart for the service of God, holy is used in a derivative sense. This is useful and defensible, so long as the emphasis is on the relationship of all such to the uncreated and unique Godhead. It leads to confusion of thought, and to superstition in practice, when the awe and reverence due to God alone are taken to be due also to what is not God.

In modern theology, particularly since the publication of Rudolf Otto's *Das Heilige* in 1917 (English trans. *The Idea of the Holy*, 1923), 'the holy' has aroused lively discussion. Otto used this term in reviving and elaborating the view that the characteristic, and essential, factor in all religious experience is non-rational awe and dread. His essay illuminated some passages in the Bible, as well as many non-scriptural accounts of religious experience.

The weaknesses in the theory are twofold. First, mere awe and dread are induced in men by experiences other than experience of supernatural reality. Second, on this theory it seems impossible to understand man's insight (which Otto shared) into the self-manifestation of God as righteous and loving, as well as 'altogether other' and sovereign. In the history of man's response to God's approach, the elements of awesome dread on the one hand, and moral reverence on the other, have undoubtedly been mixed in greatly varying proportions. The question is whether moral reverence could ever have entered into religious experience at all, if at any time 'the holy', in the sense of non-rational, awesome dread, was the only ingredient.

HOLY SCRIPTURE is a title for Christian doctrine concerning the Bible. The Bible is made up of writings grouped together in the Old and New Testaments. For some Churches it includes also a number of intertestamental books, called the Apocrypha. Merely as such, it may be treated as a collection of documents composed during the course of ten centuries or so, and in part recording traditions much older than the original writings themselves. For theology, the Bible is more than that. It is testimony to the self-disclosure and action of God in and through Jesus Christ for the salvation of men. The New Testament is Scripture in that sense. The Old Testament is also claimed as Christian Scripture, because of the way Jesus himself, the disciples, and the early Church, regarded and made use of the Jewish Scriptures.

Christian doctrine goes further. That is why 'holy' is added to 'scripture'. In its primary sense, holy is applicable to God alone. In a secondary sense, however, it is applied to whatever is associated with, or set apart for, the living God (see 'Holy'). The term Holy Scripture, then, signifies that the Bible is more than a record of revelation. It is more than testimonies to experiences of God. It is also a medium of revelation. By it God continually makes himself known to contemporary men, and addresses them.

The unique authority of the Bible as Holy Scripture is, therefore, twofold. First, in manifold ways it witnesses to the historical self-disclosure of God, and to the action of God for man's salvation. To speak of the historical self-disclosure of God does not, of course, mean that the Scriptures are history books. They include almost every kind of literary composition. The record of certain historical events is an essential part of Scripture, but by no means the whole of it. Yet each part, in its own manner, is testimony to the fact of divine revelation, and to the diverse ways in which God has declared himself. Each part is also testimony to the varied ways in which men have responded to God. Second, the Bible is found to be a contemporary medium for God's continuing self-disclosure and self-giving (see 'Word of God').

What is thus combined in the doctrine of Holy Scripture, namely, its unique authority as historical witness, and its unique authority as a contemporary medium of revelation, can be disjoined only with bad effects. Sometimes 'the theological use of the Bible' is contrasted too strongly with its 'devotional use'. To make use of the Bible as a basis for the systematic study of Christian doctrine, without continuing experience of the Bible as a medium of the living Word, leads to the most arid type of theologizing. To use the Bible for devotional purposes, without the discipline of patient study of it, is to leave open the way for pious fantasies. The doctrine of Holy Scripture is fundamental for guidance in the practice of true piety, as well as for the study of Christian doctrine as a whole. (See also 'Hermeneutics', 'Revelation', 'Myth', 'Theology'.)

HOLY SPIRIT is the name given to the third 'person' of the Trinity, who was characterized at the Second General Council (Constantinople, 381) as "the Lord and Life-giver, who proceeds from the Father, who with the Father and Son is worshipped together and glorified together, who spoke through the prophets". The Western Church modified this later, by adding what is known as the 'filioque clause', so that it read, "who proceeds from the Father and the Son". The statement as a whole indicates the main divisions of the doctrine, which is sometimes called 'pneumatology': namely, the work and the person of the Holy Spirit.

The work of the Holy Spirit, as recorded in the New Testament, is explicitly linked with what is said of it in the Old Testament. There the Spirit of God usually signifies divine energy at work: in creation, in the support of life, and in the mind of man. Divine energy was often recognized in the occurrence of the unusual, whether in men or in nature. Christian reflection on the Old Testament recognizes the work of the Holy Spirit, also, in the guiding of the history of the people of Israel, in the prophets who spoke the Word of the Lord, in the creating of piety among the Hebrews, as well as in the composing of the Old Testament writings themselves. The New Testament witnesses to experience of the Holy Spirit in the coming, life, and work of Jesus Christ; in the events of Pentecost; in the expansion of the early Church; and in abnormal gifts, as well as graces of character, given to leaders and members of Christian congregations.

Christian doctrine treats of the work of the Holy Spirit in the Christian community, in the Christian individual, and in the world. The Church is a result of the work of the Holy Spirit, both in its founding, and ever since. One way of describing the Church, indeed, is as a communion of those who jointly participate in the Holy Spirit. The Church is not only a product of the Holy Spirit: it is also an agency of the Holy Spirit. It is so, in so far as its fellowship, and its services of worship, as well as its various organizations, awaken, inform, and strengthen the faith of individuals. For the work of the Holy Spirit with individuals, see 'Sanctification'. The Church is also an agency of the Holy Spirit in so far as, illumined and energized by the Holy Spirit, it engages in its given task of mission. It is the means whereby God's rule and reign are exhibited, and forwarded, in the world. This raises, for some theologians, the question whether the Holy Spirit works only through the Church. A major consideration in any such discussion is this: the world, in the sense of communities and individuals who live without taking God into account, are part of God's created order, and within God's sovereignty. The work of the Holy Spirit, it would appear, cannot be confined to the Church and its members. Indeed, in its mission the Church is called to recognize, and to respond to, the activity of the Holy Spirit in the spirit of man, in individuals, and in community life, beyond the bounds of the Church.

The doctrine of the person of the Holy Spirit, fully developed later in trinitarian doctrine, is based on experience of the Holy Spirit's working. Testimony to the personal character of such work has already been mentioned. In the New Testament, the Spirit signifies, in some passages, a conscious purposive activity; in others, however, more than that, namely, the source of such activity. It is more reasonable to account for the former passages in the light of the latter, than the other way round. Some statements identify the Spirit with the risen Lord, but the main drift is against this. The full doctrine of a personal, divine being, in some way distinguishable from the Father and the Son, begins to emerge in several passages. They include the statement that the Holy Spirit, who comes from God, also turns towards God in intercession for Christians. (See also 'Trinity'.)

IMAGO DEI, now a technical term to express part of the Christian doctrine of man, is taken from the story of creation (Gen. 1: 26). The way it is used tends to vary according to the way in which the total doctrine is developed. Any affirmation that man is 'imago Dei', or 'made in the likeness of God', however, suggests a number of important points.

First, man's likeness to God does not properly refer to man's physical nature or appearance. In the history of doctrine, this point has not always seemed obvious. Second, the doctrine of man as 'imago Dei', taken as it is from the story of creation, emphasizes that any likeness whatever between human nature and divine nature is a gift from God. It is not, and cannot be, a human achievement. Third, to say that man was, or is, made in the likeness of God gets any meaning it may have, not from speculation about the nature of God, but from what God has disclosed himself to be, and to be doing. The supreme disclosure of God, however, is in and through Jesus Christ. Jesus Christ is the proper 'imago Dei' (cf. Col. 2: 9–10; 3: 9–10).

If likeness to God is to be understood by reference to the life, teaching, passion, and resurrection of Jesus Christ, an important fourth point must be made. So far as 'imago Dei' is applicable to any other person, it must refer principally to what man is meant to be, rather than to what now he is. In other words, man, as God's creation, has a God-given capacity for becoming a member of the kingdom of God. This capacity becomes actual, when a man responds in trust and obedience to God's gracious approach and dealings with him. No one becomes a child of God, as distinct from God's creature, merely by the fact of existing as a man (see John 1: 10–13). Interpreted in this way, 'imago Dei' carries within it the evangelical protest against those who assume spiritual privileges on account of their heredity (see Matt. 3: 9;

1 Cor. 15: 44-49). At this point, Christian doctrine is at odds with atheistic forms of humanism.

Fifth, the possibilities in man, indicated by 'made in the likeness of God', are nevertheless not merely futuristic. Man has a capacity for God here and now. Certainly man is sinful. The appeal of the Gospel, however, is to men and women as they are, in the assurance that, by virtue of the gift of being made in the likeness of God, they are capable of becoming, by God's grace, what they are meant to be. (See also 'Justification by Faith', 'Sanctification', 'Perfection'.)

Sixth, the affirmation of man as 'imago Dei' must be interpreted in more than individualistic terms. The doctrine emphasizes God's gift to each one. At the same time, its social significance is clearly brought out, when the revelation of God's nature and purposes is expressed in such words as 'love', 'the kingdom of God', 'the household of God', 'the church of God', 'the people of God'. The parables which express most vividly the care of God for each person (e.g. in Luke 15) are told against the background of the group to which each one properly belongs.

IMMANENCE AND TRANSCENDENCE are used in theology to signify the nature of the relationship of God to the world and man. Used in this way, they are not to be opposed to one another. They are strictly correlative terms.

The words, which mean literally 'indwelling' and 'surmounting', are of course spatial metaphors. Their meaning, when applied to God, is to be understood by analogy from human experience (see 'Analogy'). The maker of a musical composition, or of a poem, is other than what he makes. We may say that the musician, or poet, as the author of a sonata or a lyric, is, in relation to what he has made, 'transcendent'. At the same time, he is in every part of his composition. He is thoroughly 'immanent' in his work.

By analogy, the doctrine of creation affirms the transcendence of God in relation to the existence of all creatures whatsoever. Before they were, he is. After they come into existence, he remains other than they and, as their author, 'above' them. Following out the analogy, the doctrine of creation goes on to affirm also the immanence of God in relation to all creatures. Any significance they may have derives from their participation in God's continuing creative intention. The analogy is imperfect. For instance, not only the significance of all creatures, but also their continuance in being (unlike human productions) depends entirely upon their author. (See also 'Creation', 'Ontology'.)

The Christian doctrine of God is perverted, when either 'immanence' or 'transcendence' is used in too great isolation from the other term. This has often happened in the history of theology. When the immanence of God is unduly emphasized, theology veers in the direction of Pantheism. All beings are then apt to be regarded as no more than varieties of the being of God, without any relative independence of their own. (See also 'Creation', 'Person'.) God and Nature become almost interchangeable terms. When the transcendence of God is over-emphasized, theology veers in the direction of Deism. God is then strictly 'totally other' than the world and man, without enough regard being paid to his presence and activity at every point in the created universe (see 'Attributes of God').

JUSTIFICATION BY FAITH expresses doctrine which, at one time, aroused bitter controversy between Protestants and Roman Catholics. It still creates confusion, owing to diverse ways of interpreting its main terms. By 'justification' in the modern sense of vindicating or excusing oneself, no one can be saved before God: quite the opposite. When 'justification' is taken literally as 'made righteous', then the New Testament use of the term is not being adequately expressed (see 'Sanctification'). But New Testament usage is not being fully expressed, either, if 'justification' is taken to mean no more than 'declared righteous'.

On the basis of Biblical studies, the continuing experience of the Christian community, and the history of doctrine, it would appear that the doctrine emphasizes the following seven points. First, the salvation of any man rests upon the graciousness of God alone. Second, the graciousness of God is shown, above all, in the fact that, while men were still sinners, Christ died for them. That is not merely an event in the past. The Church proclaims, and its experience verifies the fact, that God accepts sinful men as his children, in spite of their sinfulness. (See also 'Sin', 'Salvation'.) Fourth, God's acceptance of sinners, involving as it does a personal relationship, is possible only when a man responds in trust and obedience to God's gracious invitation (see 'Person'). The invitation is made plain supremely, and uniquely, in the life, teaching, and passion of Jesus Christ. It is proclaimed by the Church. God's acceptance of sinners becomes effectual by faith, in that sense of trustful, obedient response to the proclamation of the Gospel (see 'Faith'). Fifth, such saving faith is the work of the Holy Spirit who leads a man to repentance. Repentance signifies a person's realization of his disobedience towards God; trust in the revealed love and mercy of God; and a desire to be and to live as a child of God in his household. Sixth, such change of mind and attitude may be a sudden matter, a datable conversion experience, but it need not be so. In either case, it is the ground of assurance of salvation, not as an accomplishment of his own, but as the gift of God. Seventh, by adoption into God's household while yet sinful, a man is open to God's continuous, gracious dealings with him, and thereby grows in obedience and true sonship. Such growth is associated with the use of the means of grace (see 'Grace'). These include the fellowship of the Church; the hearing of the Word of God, and receiving it, through preaching, the Scriptures, and the sacraments; and also the opportunities and duties presented in daily life.

When the doctrine is interpreted along these lines, any stark opposition between the view that 'justification' means 'declared righteous', and the view that it means 'made righteous', is overcome. This opposition was not pronounced in the early period of the Reformation movement. It grew, however, when some theologians, both Roman Catholic and Protestant, insisted on taking legalistic views. According to the legalistic view, the holy God cannot possibly accept sinful persons as his children. Before they can be accepted, they have to be made righteous (see 'Atonement'). This was in effect going back to Paul's position before he was converted.

On the other hand, in opposition to that view, some Protestants failed to make it sufficiently plain that God's acceptance of the sinful is the beginning of a new life. To be 'declared righteous' hardly does justice to that. Nor do such recent phrases as 'God's acceptance of the unacceptable'. They have to be filled out, in order to cover what Paul meant by "called to be saints", and "being saved" (see 'Sanctification').

MORAL ARGUMENTS for the existence of God, like the Cosmological and Teleological Arguments, appeal to matters of fact about the universe, but in this case to man's awareness of worth, or value. Moral arguments are sometimes confined to goodness. With other thinkers, the word 'moral' is used to include also beauty and truth. The arguments have no standing with those who believe that truth, beauty, and goodness are merely products of human mentality, individual or social – in other words, merely human conventions.

The varieties of moral arguments for the existence of God cannot be covered in a short article, nor can examples of them be presented in any complete way. The general drift, however, may be indicated in the following way. To begin with truth, the argument asks for agreement that, for example, the statement "air is lighter than water under terrestrial conditions", expresses truth whether you or I or any particular person happens to know it or not. Further, that it would still be true, even if an atom bomb wiped out the human race. That truth is not a physical reality, like air or water, and yet it is reality of a sort. Its reality subsisted before there were human beings, and would go on subsisting if there was none. Must there not be, therefore, a non-human supreme mind for whom all truths subsist?

So far as beauty is concerned, it is found in unspoiled nature. Beauty is not read into nature by human beings. They find it there. It is not to be explained entirely in utilitarian terms, such as its helpfulness in the survival of organic life. Therefore, the argument runs, the presence of beauty suggests the existence of a supreme artistic mind as creator of the universe.

So far as ethical conduct is concerned, all men are aware of an obligation to prefer what they know to be the better course of action, even if it is inconvenient, or dangerous, or directly contrary to social conventions. They vary a good deal in the ways they regard 'better' and 'worse'. They may not follow the obligation of which they are aware. The fact of such obligation however cannot be denied. Does this not suggest a supreme, divine lawgiver? And if conduct includes attitudes, desires, and ways of thinking, as well as practical deeds, does not mankind in general experience such inescapable obligations, not only to prefer goodness to badness, but also to value truth above falsehood, and beauty above ugliness – however varied may be men's notions about all these? This general fact of obligation, which cannot be explained merely on the grounds of past or present conventions, bespeaks a supreme moral being.

Even when stated much more fully, and much more carefully, such arguments are open to criticism. Supposing they can be framed to meet objections – especially the objection that values are human conventions – they still do not provide any conclusive argument for the existence of God in the way theology understands 'God'. The best they can do is, in conjunction with other arguments for the existence of God, to point in the general direction of belief in a transcendental reality, the existence of which would answer the ultimate philosophical question, 'How did anything real come to be at all?'

MYSTICISM, as a technical term, describes that kind of religious experience, usually involving a strenuous course of preparation, and open to only a minority of persons, in which, it is claimed, individuals have 'immediate' awareness of God, and ecstatic union with him. It is to be carefully distinguished from that 'sense of the presence of God' which is open to all, and a factor in faith (see 'Faith'), but is often also described as 'mystical'.

Techniques of preparation, while varying in detail, include asceticism, the exclusion from the mind of normal sense-imagery, and the suspension of thinking. They lead on to illumination, and the rapture of oneness with God. The experience is often accompanied by visions and auditions. Mystics return from their experience with a high degree of assurance as to the reality of their contact with God. They often enjoy an enhanced quality of life, marked by new-found joy and moral earnestness. Although strenuous preparation of this kind is essential, mystics agree that it does not invariably lead to the ecstasy of union with God. That is a super-added gift.

As an argument for the existence of God (see 'Empirical Arguments'), mysticism is defective. None can deny the mystic's witness to his complete assurance of the reality of God. If, however, as many do, he says that the experience cannot be put into words, then it cannot be discussed. On the other hand, should the mystic be able to discuss it, he invariably employs beliefs which he held prior to the experience. Thus, some Christian mystics confidently report their confrontation with the triune God, or the Blessed Virgin Mary. No Buddhist, or Muslim, has ever so reported, although they also report with confidence their ecstatic union with the All, or the One.

MYTH as a technical term in theology is used in three related but distinguishable ways. In the first place, it signifies out-moded beliefs concerning the world and man. The writers of the Bible, our Lord in the days of his flesh, the apostles and later

Christian teachers, undoubtedly held some beliefs about the world, about man, and about past history which we now know were defective, or altogether mistaken. Such out-moded beliefs, sometimes described as myths, present a problem about which three things must be said. First, such pre-scientific beliefs cannot be treated in theology as if they were scientifically true. Second, the language of the Bible, based on and including many pre-scientific beliefs, is nevertheless peculiarly fitted for mediating the truth of the gospel (see further below). As Jesus Christ appeared in the fullness of time in other respects – historical, religious, sociological, etc. – so also he came when a certain framework of beliefs about the world and man was ready as a most suitable medium for expressing the divine purposes. Third, it is part of the continuing theological task to re-state Scriptural testimony in terms which accord with present-day knowledge. The task is difficult because of the intimate way in which a pre-scientific framework of beliefs is bound up with the Gospel itself. Moreover, the task calls for great care, because scientific discovery, and theories based on scientific knowledge, are constantly changing.

In the second place, myth is used theologically to describe an inevitable characteristic of the language of faith (see 'Faith'). God is transcendent reality and 'altogether other' (see 'Immanence and Transcendence'). Experience of God can only be expressed in terms of experience of what is not God. Such language is thoroughly analogical (see 'Analogy'), and in part is bound to be paradoxical (see 'Paradox'). When it is described, by Bultmann for example, as mythical it is being characterized, not as untrue, but as necessarily inadequate, because it is the expression of the other-worldly and divine in terms drawn from and primarily applicable to what is of this world and human. The programme of de-mythologizing is in part to make plain the extent to which religious and theological language is inadequate, and in part to reinterpret Biblical and traditional forms of Christian thought in less inadequate ways for contemporary persons.

In the third place, but inextricably involved in what has just

43

been said, myth is sometimes applied more particularly to certain religious symbols. Verbal religious symbols are of two kinds. Some are ways of expressing religious truth which can be put in other, perhaps less poetic, ways. For instance, God's right arm is a symbol expressing divine activity, skill, and power. Some however cannot be translated into other words: for example, God is love. Love as an untranslatable symbol of supernatural reality is describable, in this third usage of the term, as a myth.

NATURAL THEOLOGY is a term used in several ways. Sometimes it stands for the orderly study of beliefs implied in 'natural religion', as distinct from any particular, organized religion. What such natural religion might be, indeed whether there is any such thing, is open to question. Sometimes, natural theology is an alternative title for 'rational theology', or 'transcendental theology'. In this sense, it means the attempt to establish the truth of certain statements about God, by reasoning from self-evident truths. Whether there are any truths strictly self-evident (even for example 2 + 2 = 4) is nowadays widely questioned. Usually, however, natural theology is an alternative name for 'metaphysical theology', or 'philosophical theology', and signifies the attempt to reach a high degree of reasonable certitude as to the existence of God, his nature, and relationship to the universe, by reasoning from what can be known about the world and man, including religious experience (see 'Philosophy of Religion', with its reference to other articles).

The term, natural theology, implies a sharp contrast with 'revealed theology'. The latter is usually intended to signify the orderly study of truths which could not possibly be discovered by human reasoning, but which have been disclosed by God himself. The doctrine of the Trinity is an example. Some theologians deny that there is any such thing as 'revealed theology'. Others regard 'natural theology' as a contradiction in terms. Others again hold that certain basic truths, such as the existence of God, can be established by the methods of 'natural theology', but that for fuller knowledge of God it is necessary to have recourse to 'revealed theology'.

The use of 'natural' and 'revealed' in this way is questionable. All theology is natural, in the sense that it is a human enterprise. On the other hand, all theology, as distinct from theistic philosophy, is concerned, directly or indirectly, with revelation, in the sense of divine self-disclosure. (See also 'Revelation', 'Theology'.)

ONTOLOGICAL ARGUMENTS for the existence of God, associated especially with Anselm (1033–1109) and Descartes (1596–1650), but now once more a lively topic of discussion, begin with a description of God on which agreement may be assumed. They go on to show that this very description logically forces one to hold that God exists. The notion of God, as Anselm put it, is "that than which no greater can be conceived", or, as Descartes put it, a "being supremely perfect". The further step in the argument may be in one of several, rather different, directions. It might be: to exist is greater, or more perfect, than not to exist; therefore, God exists. Or: what exists without any dependence on anything else whatever for its existence is greater, or more perfect, than what does depend for existence on something else; therefore, God not only exists, but his existence is necessary existence. Or: that which cannot be thought of as not existing is more perfect than what can be thought of as, sometime in the past or in the future, not existing; therefore, God cannot be thought of as not existing; God necessarily exists.

Those who advocated the argument as a compelling one hoped it would carry the same kind of immediate conviction as the statement that the three angles of a triangle equal two right-angles. They had to point out, of course, that they were not talking about some finite thing, like an island. You can think, as Anselm's opponent, Gaunilo, said, of a perfect island, but that does not

45

prove that it exists. God is not perfect, however, in the sense of being the most perfect of his kind. He is the only one, and he is the infinite one.

The most serious attack upon the argument was that of Kant (1724–1804). The statement about the angles of a triangle is compelling. It does not prove, however, that any perfect triangle exists. From the notion of a perfect triangle, it follows of necessity that its angles would total 180 degrees. So, from the notion of God as a perfect being, the notion of his existence follows. But it does not follow that he actually exists. That would have to be demonstrated in some way other than by reasoning.

The ontological argument has seemed to many impressive. It strikes others as absurd. It is worth remembering that Anselm's statement was made in a devotional setting. It was put in the context of faith. The preface to the argument includes these words: 'And so, O Lord, since thou givest understanding to faith, give me to understand – as far as thou knowest it to be good for me – that thou dost exist, as we believe, and that thou art what we believe thee to be." God is for him a proper name (see 'God'), with all that is implied by that fact, before ever he analyses the 'concept' of God. The ontological argument still has life in it for those who, on religious or indeed on philosophical grounds, cannot escape the conviction that, beyond human experience or thought concerning finite things, there must be a reality so perfect that we cannot think of it as not existing. In other words, the force of the argument lies in what is implied by the original title of Anselm's little book: *Faith seeking Understanding*.

ONTOLOGY is the doctrine of Being. It was discussed by the early Greek philosophers, but it has played an important part in both ancient and modern theology. The use of 'Being' has varied a good deal. On the one hand, it is contrasted with 'Becoming', or change of some sort. On the other hand, it is contrasted with 'Nothing'. In both cases, it is used to signify what is real, as distinct from what may falsely be taken as real. According to the first view, only that which is changeless is really real. According to the second, reality is a combination of what exists in time, and is therefore changeable, and what subsists irrespective of time, and is therefore changeless.

Over a long period, the theological discussion of Being has tried to reconcile the Christian doctrine of God with the philosophical doctrine of Being as changeless reality (see 'Eternity'). One reason for recurrent objections to the influence of philosophy on theology, is that such an attempt cannot be harmonized with Biblical testimony as a whole to the self-manifestation of the living God. According to that witness, God is working his purpose out: he can be characterized in such terms as creator, sovereign, one who is righteous and loving. Changelessness is not compatible with what such terms imply, even when the inevitable limitations of human speech about God have been taken into account. (See also 'Analogy', 'Myth'.)

The view that Being is the opposite of 'Nothing' is easier to harmonize with the Christian doctrines of God, the world, and man. Indeed, it sheds some light on Christian doctrine. God is Being-itself, in the sense of perfect reality. He is, and he is unchangeably good. All else that is, was created out of nothing (see 'Creation'). Not only so, all that was created was good. Without some participation in the Being of God, everything that exists would be, not only worthless, but nothing. Sin, as estrangement from God, is therefore a dire threat to the Being of man. Redemption is the removal of that threat, and through Christ's atoning work man may be saved into eternal life (cf. Rom. 6, especially *v.* 23; and see 'Atonement').

PARADOX means, literally, against current opinion. Often it is used to describe statements which are just absurd. In theology, however, it is used in a rather different way. It is applied to doctrinal statements which, if taken literally, are

47

self-contradictory or nonsensical, but which have to be put that way, in order to express truth concerning God. For example, the doctrine that God created all things out of nothing is apparently absurd. The theologian describes it as paradox. In this example, the paradoxical statement is not designed to avoid difficulties in speaking about God as Creator, but to show them up. The difficulty is, that the following points have to be made at one and the same time: the world is not to be identified with God; the world owes its existence to God; but the world is not made of some neutral, or evil, stuff which had some sort of existence, independent of God, before creation. Those points, and others, have to be made, if faith and reflection upon it are adequately to be expressed (see 'Creation'). The only brief way of declaring this, and facing the difficulties, is to use a paradoxical statement. Other examples are to be found in the doctrine of Scripture, and the doctrine of the Incarnation. The Bible is the work of human beings, from cover to cover, yet it is all the work of God. Jesus Christ is genuinely human, yet genuinely divine. Non-paradoxical language is unable to state what faith cannot deny. (See also 'Holy Scripture', 'Christology'.)

Unavoidable paradox, in the statement of truth about God, must be distinguished from avoidable self-contradiction. The former is the result of serious and strenuous reflection; the latter comes from muddle-headedness. Paradox arises from the nature of theology as human language about God; avoidable self-contradiction arises from the weakness of theologians. For further notes on the difficulty of using language about God, see also the articles on 'Analogy', 'Myth', and 'Symbol'.

PERFECTION plays an important part in the doctrines of God and salvation. In the former, the term is used to express the completeness in every respect of the nature of God. This implies that the Being of God is essentially beyond human understanding; and it affirms that any lack which can possibly be conceived by man is untrue of God. God is 'infinite' in that double sense. Theological debate tends to revolve around the question whether change of any kind whatsoever is a limitation, or defect. (See also 'Eternity', 'Ontology'.) The term 'perfections' has long been used as an equivalent to 'attributes'. By some modern theologians, e.g. Karl Barth, it is still so preferred. (See also 'Attributes of God', 'God'.)

In the doctrine of salvation, theologians have used perfection in more than one way. The emphasis may be on freedom from sin. In that case, the notion of perfection will vary in accordance with the way in which 'sin' is being used (see 'Sin'). On the other hand, the emphasis may be on positive goodness, particularly perfect love. All this bears upon a difficult question, which is raised in the New Testament itself, and which has been discussed, from a very early period, in the history of theology. Is perfection a possibility for Christians in this life, and therefore something to be expected, or something to be striven after as an obligation? (See Matt. 5: 48; I John 1: 8 and 3: 9; Phil. 3: 12 –16.)

In the second century, some influential theologians (e.g. Basilides and Valentinus) used the pre-Christian notion that the spirit of man was imprisoned in his body, and that salvation meant release from this bondage. They taught that secret knowledge (gnosis), imparted by Christ, gave in this life complete emancipation from the flesh. Those who were illumined in this way were perfect here and now. Reacting against such views, and appalled by the immorality which in practice often went along with them, other teachers (Pelagius, born about 370, and his followers), having denied the doctrine of original sin (see 'Sin'), taught that perfection of character was indeed possible in this life; but it was to be achieved by moral education, and by discipline. Their great opponent, Augustine (354–430), like Thomas Aquinas (about 1225–74), interpreted perfection as perfect love. They believed that perfect love was possible for a few, but they strongly denied that it was possible for most Christians. Augustine held, indeed, that any progress whatever in holiness depended upon a man's receiving that divine gift of 'sanctifying grace' which is available through the sacrament of Holy Communion. (See also 'Grace', 'Sacraments'.) He sharply discounted the value of moral effort, apart from that gift.

Perfection in the sense of mystical union with God is possible for a few, according to those who advocate the way of negation and purgation which leads up to it (see 'Mysticism'). But this, and all other views that perfection was possible in man's present life, were strenuously denied by the Reformers of the sixteenth and seventeenth centuries. For them, man's spiritual warfare and his imperfection continue until the day of his death. The reason lies in the Reformers' doctrine of sin. They regarded sin as any transgression, or any coming short, of the will of God, whether known by a man, or not. In this respect, their doctrine reflected the manifold nature of Biblical language about sin (see 'Sin'). No man knows the whole mind of God, or can know it, and therefore no man can possibly be perfect in this life.

Pietists disagreed with the Reformers, and their view was shared by some Quakers, who believed that, by openness to the 'inner light', and by constant following of it, a Christian might be freed from sinfulness. Among Protestants, however, it is especially with John Wesley (1703–91) that the doctrine of perfection is connected. Sinners who have been justified by faith through Christ, not only may, but should, strive to become perfect, in the sense of being controlled entirely by the spirit of love. Wesley's use of 'sin' is, on the whole, different from that of the earlier Reformers. When 'original sin' has been dealt with, in the case of any man, by the application to himself of the atoning work of Jesus Christ, to sin means to offend voluntarily against what the Christian knows of God's will. In other words, 'sin' means 'culpable sin'. With the aid of the Holy Spirit, this need not be. Wesley never claimed perfection for himself. It can be achieved, however, and, he would add, it has been achieved by a few. (See also 'Sanctification', 'Justification by Faith'.)

PERSON, a term used in widely differing ways during the history of theology, signifies primarily the unique status, in the natural order, of every human being. Each human being is in part the product of biological evolution, of history, of his present environment, and of his own past life so far. Essentially, however, he is more than that. He is capable, to some extent, of making decisions which are not to be accounted for entirely by any, or all, of these factors. No being in which this unique capacity is completely absent could rightly be called a human being. Any non-human being which has this capacity can properly be described, by analogy, as at least personal.

The human capacity for making such decisions is not exercised without any motive whatever. In making decisions, however, a person is one who can consider appeals, or pressures, to act in this way or in that, and in deciding one way or the other he does so, in some measure, as we say, "on his own responsibility". This is the double significance of 'freedom': negatively, not entirely bound to act in accordance with pressures from environment, from other beings, from instinctual drives, or from subconscious motives; positively, able to some extent to exercise decision as to alternative future courses of action, in the light of one's own evaluation of them.

Without attempting a full discussion, four matters call for mention. First, as distinct from organisms which are conscious, a person is self-conscious. Second, there can be no such being as a person, except in mutual relations with other persons: self-consciousness, for example, arises in the course of such relationships. Third, the terms 'act' and 'action', used in connection with decisions, include thoughts and feelings, as well as 'practical' deeds. Fourth, no human being is entirely personal: he has affinities with non-personal creatures, and appears to be motivated in ways similar to some of theirs; he is far from being self-conscious; and the degree to which, in any situation, he is in fact free to decide, is greatly limited by all the factors mentioned earlier, including the consequences of his own earlier choices.

This use of the term 'person' harmonizes with the Christian

doctrine of man. **Man** is created as essentially a responsible being, in the sense of 'able to respond' to God, and also himself 'accountable' for the kind of response he makes, with its consequences. It is God's purpose in creation to make a community of persons, his kingdom, or household. God's mighty acts of redemption are to deliver men as individuals from the lack of freedom, which their own wrong decisions, and the wrong choices of others, in the society to which they belong, have entailed. Those acts of redemption are, also, to bring men into the fully personal society of those who are reconciled to the living God (cf. Heb. 2: 10; and see 'Creation', 'Salvation', 'Reconciliation').

Historically, 'person' has been used in various ways. At times it meant, for example, a human being with legal rights, a description which did not apply to every human being; or, the part which an actor might play on the stage – the sense in which, for a long period, 'person' has been used, by analogy, for the roles of members of the divine Trinity; or, the 'soul' of a human being; or, a 'rational' being. The modern existentialist concern with human beings is, in no small measure, a revolt against all earlier inadequate views, especially the rationalist view, as to what it means to be a human being (see 'Existentialism', 'Substance').

PHILOSOPHY OF RELIGION, for which alternative but less accurate titles (such as 'religious philosophy', 'natural theology', 'philosophical theology') are sometimes used, is properly describable as philosophical concern with religion. As such, it clearly has a place in philosophical studies. However, if theology is in part an engagement with current non-Christian convictions, philosophy of religion has a rightful place in theological studies as well.

It may be divided into two parts. The first is concerned with the nature of religion. The second is concerned with the validity of religious claims to be dealing with an invisible, supernatural reality.

52

The study of the nature of religion follows two lines of enquiry. One is the psychological study of religious mentality and behaviour. This is undertaken by the methods – so far as they are applicable – used in the general study of human behaviour and mentality. It includes the application to religious experience of what is known about subconscious mental activity, the nature and importance of primary mental drives ('instincts'), the nature of feeling, and so on. For the philosopher of religion, these enquiries are valuable in several ways. They show, for example, that religious experiencing does not make use of some special faculty of the mind. What makes it distinctive is the fact that it refers to, and claims to be a dealing with, a worshipful arbiter of man's blessedness and woe. Again, the psychological study of religion helps in the evaluation of arguments from religious experience to the reality of what is worshipped (see last paragraph below). Again, this study gives more general help in assessing the strength and weakness of theories about religion which are based upon psychology.

The seond line of enquiry into the nature of religion is a historical study of the various forms of religion. Different organized religions display a variety of interpretation of what is taken to be sacred reality. To examine these interpretations, to classify them, to see if there are lines of development in them, and so on, is valuable preparation for dealing with the crucial questions (see below) which have to be considered in philosophy of religion.

Study of the nature of religion prepares the way for the major concern of philosophy of religion, which is with questions of validity and truth. Are religious claims about invisible, supernatural reality valid claims? Are the beliefs which express religious experience true? In other words, philosophy of religion is mainly concerned with the knowledge-claims of religion (see 'Epistemology'). Under this heading, subjects for discussion include the following. First, the dismissal of religious experience, in all its forms, as illusory. Second, explanations of the human situation which claim to be completely adequate, without bringing

53

in the concept of God at all. Such explanations are sometimes called 'anti-theistic theories'. Third, linguistic arguments, which question the meaningfulness of the statements in which religious beliefs are expressed. Fourth, empirical arguments in support of belief in the existence of God (for these, see 'Empirical Arguments'). Fifth, rationalistic arguments in support of theistic belief. These include the ontological, cosmological, moral, and teleological arguments (see articles under each of these headings. See also 'Theology', 'God'.)

PREDESTINATION is used, in a more general sense, to signify the belief that God's purposes, including the destiny of mankind, are unchangeable, even from before the creation of the universe. It is also used, in a more specific way, to signify the doctrine that God has fore-ordained particular persons to salvation, and others to perdition.

Predestination, in the more general sense, is doctrine acceptable to most Christians. The righteous, loving purposes of God, manifested supremely in and through Jesus Christ, are unchangeable (see 'Eternity'). This is not to be confused with fatalism. It does not rule out the possibility that some persons will fail to respond to God's disclosed purposes, or will reject them. (See also 'Imago Dei', 'Person'.)

In a more specific sense, predestination is one answer to problems raised by certain matters of fact. For example, many human beings have never been confronted effectually with the good news of God's saving purposes for them. Again, still fewer have been offered the gospel of God's saving purpose in Jesus Christ. Again, some who have been confronted with the Christian gospel have responded to it gladly; but others have turned away. How can such matters of fact be reconciled with belief in the sovereignty of God?

There are four possible answers. First, God in his sovereign purpose has determined that only some persons shall be saved.

54

Whether this or that particular person is included among them, however, depends upon whether he responds, in trustful obedience, to what he knows of God's will, or not. Second, God desires, not some only, but all men to be saved; nevertheless, his sovereign purpose created men capable of accepting or rejecting God's good purpose for them. Third, it is God's sovereign purpose that every one shall be saved, and eventually this shall be accomplished. Fourth, it is God's sovereign purpose that only a certain number of persons shall be saved, and they will.

This fourth answer is incorporated in the specific doctrine of predestination. Whether it is true cannot be determined by quoting isolated Biblical passages. They can be offset by other passages in the Bible. The theological task is to consider how Christian doctrine as a whole bears upon this particular teaching. As we have seen, it consists of two parts, each of which calls for careful attention.

First, it affirms that, from all eternity, God has decreed that only some persons shall be saved. This implies that, from all eternity, God has determined that others shall not be saved. Indeed, some variations of the doctrine declared that, for some, God has decreed from all eternity the fate of everlasting torment. Does this part of the doctrine, in any way of stating it, harmonize with what God has disclosed of himself, and his will for men, according to the testimony of the New Testament as a whole?

Second, it affirms that those persons whom God has determined beforehand to save shall be saved. All Christians would agree that no one can be saved, except through the gracious initiative, and continual aid, of God. The doctrine is right, in so far as it reflects that profound conviction. But can anyone be saved, apart from personal response to what he knows of God's will? Is not a man's personal decision needed, as well as the will of God, if he is finally to be saved, at least in the way salvation is set forth in the New Testament? (See also 'Universalism', 'Salvation', 'Election'.)

PROVIDENCE is the doctrine which brings together Christian teaching on the sovereignty of God in relation to the world and man, on the one hand, and Christian teaching about the love of God, on the other.

The 'sovereignty' of God is an analogical way of speaking (see 'Analogy'). It is drawn from human relationships in an ancient Oriental setting. Ideal monarchy, in such a setting, suggests absolute power over subject persons and property, and supreme authority in the making of law, together with wisdom and complete righteousness in its administration. The 'love' of God, on the other hand, is interpreted by Christians in terms of the actions, attitudes, sayings, and passion of Jesus Christ.

By refusing to separate, indeed by resolutely keeping in mind together, the sovereignty and the love of God, Christian doctrine concerning God's ways with the world and man is delivered from two major sources of error: from sentimental interpretations of divine love, and from crude, impersonal applications of the notion of omnipotence (see 'Attributes of God'). Nevertheless, in doing so, it is compelled to face serious problems, which are raised by human experience of appalling desolations and distress. The problems are felt in relation to all mankind. They become even more acute, because of the woeful experiences of many who have put their faith in the God and Father of Jesus Christ.

The doctrine of providence may be divided into two parts. The first, entitled divine preservation, sets out God's activity in relation to the natural order. It emphasizes God's continual, all-embracing relationship with what he has created: God is nowhere, and at no time, an absentee God. It also stresses the relative independence which God has given to the natural order: it is his creation, and God is not simply to be identified with nature. Further, the natural order exhibits regularities, or reliable sequences (what used to be called 'laws of nature'). These are meaningful for God's ways with man, as part of the created order, and consequently for the ways in which man must order his life within it. Some of these regularities, being not yet fully understood by man, appear to him as inexplicable disasters, e.g. earthquakes (see 'Creation').

The second part of the doctrine, entitled divine government, sets out God's ways in relation to human history. It emphasizes God's continual, all-embracing relationship with men in societies, and as individuals. No community, and no individual, are outside God's sovereign, loving purposes. It stresses also the relative independence which God has given to men (see 'Imago Dei'). Further, the course of human history exhibits, in some measure, the reliable sequence of human actions and their inevitable consequences – what is sometimes called a moral order. That is so, the doctrine affirms, although the prosperity of the wicked, and the sufferings of the just, make it difficult in every age to discern a moral order in human affairs, without some misgivings. Such doubts are intensified, not lessened, by the Christian affirmation that God at times, and in particular cases, intervenes to set aside both 'laws of nature' and 'moral consequences'. If God may 'miraculously' intervene to save some from disaster, or difficulty, why does he not, out of his sovereign compassion, do so for others? (See 'Predestination.')

In developing the doctrine of providence, Christian theology is unable to limit the sovereignty of God, by putting all the blame for unjust suffering upon a rival, demonic being who is co-eternal with God (see 'Sin'). Nor may it take refuge in the theory that, because God is sovereign over all, whatever is is right. More positively, while recognizing the limitations of human insight and understanding (cf. Luke 13: 1–5), theology looks for clearer light on the problem from an interpretation of the passion and death of Jesus Christ. For in those events, whatever else is involved, supreme compassionate innocence is afflicted by unjust wickedness. Yet in those very events is manifested also the greatest act of God's sovereign love (see 'Atonement').

E

RECONCILIATION means the act, or the result, of the overcoming of estrangement between God and man. The New Testament speaks of men being reconciled to God, but not of God being reconciled to men. This suggests that, so far as the New Testament is concerned, to effect reconciliation needs no change in the attitude of God to men. His righteous mercy and love towards them are steadfast. What is required, however, is a change in the attitude of men to God. To bring about that change is the purpose of Christ's atoning work. The doctrine of reconciliation, therefore, presupposes, or is closely linked with, three other doctrines: the doctrine of the divine creation of man for fellowship with God (see 'Imago Dei'); the doctrine of sin, for sinfulness is the cause of estrangement between God and man (see 'Sin'); and the doctrine of atonement (see 'Atonement').

The range of reconciliation as a changed attitude to God, brought about by the work of Christ, is wide. It includes a man's acceptance of the natural world as instrumental to God's purposes, despite the profound difficulties created by man's experience of some of its features (see 'Providence'). It includes a denial that the natural order, or any part of it, is of final worth. So far as his fellow-men are concerned, reconciliation demands a man's acceptance of them, whoever they are and whatever their condition, as made in the image of God, and persons for whom Christ died. Nevertheless, it signifies also a willingness to deny the claims of other men and women upon us, not only those dearest to us, but also the most aggressive and powerful, whenever their claims are incompatible with the known claims of God. So far as his own life and condition are concerned, reconciliation includes a man's acceptance, without repining or envy, of those limitations which he cannot change, or cannot change with a good conscience. Reconciliation includes a willingness to subordinate his own convenience, desires, or even continuance in life, to the claims of God.

The theological significance of reconciliation is not only wide: it is also essentially active. It is not to be understood, as so often in popular usage, in terms of passive submissiveness. After all, the doctrine is based on a conviction that God takes the initiative, and is always graciously active, in dealing with those who are estranged from him. The man who is reconciled to God is called to be active in using the natural world as the handiwork of God, and the agency of his good purposes. Reconciliation to God impels a man to be zealous also in serving his neighbours, as the objects of God's loving care, and to be to them the servant of God's will. In reliance on God's help and leading (see 'Holy Spirit'), he will actively employ whatever capacities he has in the worship and service of God. (See also 'Creation', 'Grace', 'Salvation'.)

REVELATION as a theological term may refer, either to God's act of disclosing, or to the contents of what God has disclosed. In the first sense, theology discusses the means, or media, whereby divine revealing takes place. Among those mentioned in the Bible, for example, some are physical: such as, the beauty and orderliness of nature, storms, the casting of lots. Some are psychic: such as, dreams, visions, ecstatic states of mind. Some are events in history which, like the physical and psychic media, appear to be beyond the control of man.

Revelation in the second sense, what God discloses to men, is often contrasted with what men discover about God through reasoning. Human reasoning, it is said, can discover that God exists; the triune nature of God, however, could be known only by supernatural revelation. The validity of this contrast has been questioned (see 'Natural Theology'). All theologians agree that God has made himself, and his purposes, known in part to men. They further agree that the fullest revelation is to be found in Jesus Christ, the primary written testimony to whom is given in the Bible. Some of them question, however, whether the finite mind of man could possibly discover even the existence of God, or anything at all about him, unless God took the initiative in revealing himself. Again, are not all statements whatsoever about

59

God, human ways of expressing the significance of man's encounter with the living God? Or, are some statements 'direct' communications from God? Those who take the former view would agree that human attempts in the Bible and in the Church to express God's confrontation with men are 'inspired'; but they would add, that being conditioned by the thought-forms and language of their time, they need reinterpretation and re-statement in each succeeding age (see 'Myth').

SACRAMENTS are 'means of grace'. Theological discussion begins with agreement on this description, but thereafter is largely controlled by diverse convictions regarding the meaning of grace (see 'Grace').

The word 'sacrament' is not a Biblical word, but a Latin translation of the Greek 'mysterion'. This at once suggests the need for a certain diffidence in discussion: we are dealing with what are recognized to be 'mysteries'. No doubts or difficulties are to be avoided. Yet, as even the forceful and clear-headed Calvin declared, there are matters here, where even the appearance of bland assurance is out of place. Another requisite for proper discussion of the sacraments is this: convictions about the sacraments should be consistent with those which have been reached about God, the world, and man, in the light of Biblical witness as a whole to the teaching, deeds, and passion of Jesus Christ.

Although difficulties have been found in 'proving' from the Scriptures that Jesus Christ gave the sacraments to his Church (as well as in reaching agreement on the number of them), nevertheless the main streams of Christian tradition agree in affirming the 'dominical institution' of the sacraments of Baptism and the Lord's Supper (or Eucharist, or Mass, or Holy Communion). They do so on Scriptural grounds, and because of the primitive practice of the Church. Dominical institution however is interpreted in more than one way: it may be taken to mean the Lord's providing, or commanding, or commending, them.

60

The task of theology is to try and make plain what, in so doing, was our Lord's intention. The outward ritual acts – the use of water, or of bread and wine – do not bear their meaning openly, or in such a way that it could be read off by anyone just looking on. On the contrary, they will be seriously misunderstood, and even within the Christian community have been misunderstood, when the administration of the sacraments is disjoined from proclamation of the mind of Christ.

If the administration of the sacraments lacks distinctively Christian significance apart from instruction and preaching, in what way are the sacraments special (indeed, as the main Christian traditions hold, indispensable) means of grace? Is there a "secret virtue" (Calvin) in them? Over and above the verbal ministry of the Word, there is at any rate an added virtue. The profoundest things in personal relationships cannot be expressed in words; they can only be expressed, if expressible at all, in actions. As Augustine put it, the sacraments are the visible Word. In these means of grace, there is a power to elicit and confirm faith, which supplements, even while it is conjoined with, verbal proclamation of the Gospel (see 'Word of God').

Other matters which a full theological treatment of the sacraments must include are these: the relationship between the elements used in the sacraments, and that which they represent (for notes on Transubstantiation, and Consubstantiation, see 'Substance'); the relationship between the effectiveness of the sacraments and the manner of administering them, or the character of the celebrant; the sacraments as offerings to God, as well as occasions for receiving his gifts; the sacraments as professions of faith, or means of evangelism.

SALVATION is used theologically in more than one way. It may mean the act of saving; for example, "Christ's salvation of the world." It may also mean the one by whom this is done; for example, "Christ is your salvation." For these two topics, see 'Atonement,' and 'Christology'. In this article, we are concerned with a third use of the term, namely, the state or condition of being saved; for example, "In Christ is our salvation."

Salvation implies a situation from which man is to be rescued, and a condition of blessedness into which he is to be brought. In such general terms, salvation is a feature of all religious promises and aspiration. Distinctively Christian doctrine claims to declare the truth of which all other doctrines are but partial, or mistaken, statements. It is based on the supreme and final self-disclosure of God in and through Jesus Christ, together with the preparation for it, to which the Bible testifies.

Man's highest good is to be now, and for ever, a member of the kingdom, or household, of God. (See also 'Imago Dei', 'Reconciliation'.) The full significance of such language is admittedly beyond man's understanding (cf. 1 Cor. 2: 9 ff; 13: 12). That from which man has to be rescued is estrangement from God, and God's gracious way of dealing with it is by Jesus Christ the Saviour. (See also 'Sin', 'Atonement'.) Salvation, which thus has a beginning in the appropriation of the benefits of Christ's passion, and a goal in blessedness beyond our present capacity to conceive, is a life illumined and energized by the working of the Holy Spirit. According to some theologians, this life may in principle be perfected on earth, but according to others cannot here reach perfection. (See also 'Sanctification', 'Perfection'.)

Christian doctrine emphasizes throughout that salvation is God's gracious gift. In view of its personal character, however, it demands also man's response in trust and obedience (see 'Justification by Faith'; cf. Phil. 2: 12–13). While salvation is personal, and concerns persons one by one, it is not individualistic. It is always to be understood in terms of a redeemed society. The community of Christ's people on earth, like the people of God under the old covenant, enjoy something of the joy of the redeemed even now, but they are the agency of the Holy Spirit for the forwarding of God's saving work among men. (See also 'Covenant', 'Election', 'Holy Spirit'.)

SANCTIFICATION is used of the process whereby the Christian becomes more and more holy. In this connection, 'holy' has the combined sense of freedom from sin, and perfect love towards God. Sanctification is also used to describe the completion of that process, a completion which some regard as realizable in this life, but others regard as possible only after death (see 'Perfection').

Although sanctification, in the first sense, signifies being made both increasingly free from sin, and also more perfectly loving towards God, in actual usage the emphasis tends to fall upon one or the other. When freedom from sin is chiefly in mind, it is important to distinguish between the various meanings of sin (see 'Sin'). In the view of those who hold some form of the doctrine of 'original sin', a beginning in the process of sanctification becomes possible, because of the atoning work of Jesus Christ; that beginning becomes actual, whenever a person appropriates the benefits of Christ's passion; and this redemption, or deliverance, from original sin is marked by baptism. Whether they hold the doctrine of 'original sin' or not, and whatever view they take of baptism, most theologians agree on this point: no one who has been reconciled to God through Christ (see 'Atonement', 'Reconciliation') has finished with sin, in the sense of transgression of God's will. Transgression may be either unwitting, or wilful. It may be the doing of what is wrong, or failing to do what is right. Sanctification signifies growing obedience to God, in an equally comprehensive sense: greater alertness to learn God's will, and increasing compliance with it. In all this, the doctrine of sanctification emphasizes the need for openness to the gift of the illumination, and energizing power, of the Holy Spirit, as well as the need for self-discipline.

When the emphasis in sanctification is put, not so much on freedom from sin, but rather upon growth in love towards God, and therefore also in love towards one's neighbour, the essential gift of the Holy Spirit's light and energy, and the requirement of Christian responsibility, are again held together.

Theologians differ about both the gift and the task involved in

63

sanctification. First, in what way is the gift of new life, through the Holy Spirit, to be obtained? For some, the forgiveness of sins committed after appropriation of the benefits of Christ's atoning work is dependent upon confession to a priest of the Church, and suitable acts of penance. This will be followed by the gift of fresh 'grace' imparted through the sacrament of Holy Communion (see 'Grace'). For others, forgiveness is freely available upon sincere repentance and confession to God, whether in private, or spoken in the presence of another person, or in corporate worship. The gift of the Holy Spirit is given to the penitent sinner, as part of the new life of a justified sinner (see 'Justification by Faith'). The assurance of this is proclaimed, both in the preaching of the Word of God, and in the observance of the sacrament. (See also 'Word of God', 'Sacraments'.)

Second, in what manner of life is increasing love towards God and one's neighbour to be exercised? There is general agreement that sanctification, in that sense, reveals itself in ever-growing freedom from the domination of mundane affairs. A long tradition, however, regards it as best achieved by separation, as far as possible, from such affairs, including normal social relationships. A life of praying, meditation, and charitable works, lived either alone, or in a community of like-minded persons, bound together under a code of discipline, is then claimed to be, for some at least, the best way of making progress in sanctification, and service of the world. Others hold that sanctification involves the practice of the love of God, and of one's neighbour, amid the business and human relationships of the world. Such a life must be supported by the disciplines and privileges of private piety and corporate worship. With God's help, such sanctification is possible for all, and is required from all, who have been justified by faith. (See also 'Salvation', 'Reconciliation'.)

SIN is strictly a religious term, and signifies a wrong relationship with God. The reference to God, however, may be indirect.

It is proper to speak of sinning against one's neighbour, or sinning against oneself, because some attitudes towards men are an affront to God.

The Christian doctrine of sin takes into account (1) the variety of Hebrew and Greek words in the Bible, which can be translated by the single word 'sin'; (2) the occasional personifications of 'Sin' in the Bible (e.g. Gen. 4: 7; Rom. 5: 12) which, if taken literally, may obscure the fact that there is no such entity as sin, only sinful personal beings; (3) the distinction between 'sin' and 'sins', the latter indicating manifestations of sin in particular acts and attitudes; (4) the bearing upon the subject of growing knowledge about extra-conscious motivation, and feelings of guilt.

So far as the nature of sin is concerned, Christian doctrine describes it concisely as disobedience towards God. Disobedience, however, has a wide range of meaning. First, disobedience may be deliberate, or culpable. Second, through ignorance of God's will, it may be unwitting. The Biblical emphasis falls heavily upon culpable disobedience, or guilty sin; but unwitting transgression is also described as sin. Third, disobedience may mean not being on the alert to find out the will of God, an attitude described in such terms as dullness of heart, or sloth.

Christian doctrine is concerned, not only with the nature, but also with the origin of sin. Here, two questions must be distinguished. First, how does sin originate in each person now? In part, as said already, it is due to man's finitude. Each person does wrong to God through ignorance. It is blameworthy, however, to the extent to which, in any particular case, a person's ignorance is itself his fault. Disobedience is wilful, on the other hand, when a person takes no notice of, or rejects, what he consciously knows of God's holy, loving purposes. In developing Christian doctrine on both these matters, the theologian is helped by a critical and discerning use of the results of psychological science.

The second question is this: How did wilful sin originate at all

65

in the human race? This cannot be a historical question. Nevertheless, Christian doctrine continues to find in the first of the two stories of The Fall (Gen. 3 and 6) suggestions of value. First, men are responsible beings in a double sense: they are capable of recognizing, and responding to, God's will; but they also have a capacity to go against what they know of God's will, and are accountable for such disobedience. Second, God is not the author of sin, even if God "according to his wise and holy purposes was pleased to permit our first parents to sin". This is a reminder that the Christian doctrine of sin is incomplete, until it has been developed in harmonious conjunction with the doctrines of grace and salvation. Third, in every human being there is a bias towards wilful sin. Fourth, Christian doctrine has to give full weight to the fact that one sinner influences another. While each one is a responsible being (see above), each one is bound up with others in such a way that it is justifiable to speak of a kingdom of sin.

SUBSTANCE may be used both of impersonal, and of personal, beings. In both cases, it has played an important part in theological discussion. It is primarily a philosophical term. Some theologians regard its use in theology as doing nothing but harm. To understand certain crucial theological debates, however, it is necessary to be familiar with some of the ways in which it has been used.

To do justice to the subject would require a lengthy historical review. In brief, however, it begins with the question, 'What is it which makes anything really what it is?' (see 'Ontology'). A ball, for example, has a certain shape, size, colour, and so on. But all these qualities do not add up to the ball. What else is there? The notion of substance provided an answer. But what is substance? A very ancient answer was this: substance is the pattern, or form, of all the qualities, and is real in a way they are not; the pattern persists, even if the colour, or any, or all, of the qualities should change. Another answer, which held the field for a long time,

66

was that substance is the stuff which underlies all the qualities. They belong to the stuff, but it is not itself a quality. It cannot therefore be perceived; it is a mysterious something. Sometimes it was described as 'matter'. The classical terms, however, were 'substance', for the underlying stuff, and 'accidents', for the qualities. The notion of such an underlying something was rejected by some thinkers, including Kant. He put forward an alternative view. The factor which unifies all the qualities of a thing is not something else belonging to the thing; it is the built-in, organizing activity of the person who perceives them.

What, then, makes a person, as distinct from a thing, really what he is? He too is more than all the descriptive qualities which can be said about him. The term 'soul' has often been used to signify the substance of a person. The soul is also a mysterious something that cannot be perceived. In more recent times, the term 'pure ego' has been preferred. Behind the use of such terms is the awareness each one has that, despite changes in body and disposition, circumstances and mental capacities, he remains himself. In such conviction of his self-identity, each person's memory plays an important part. But even the fact of serious loss of memory (amnesia), and instances of 'split', or 'multiple', personality, have not been able to dislodge a general conviction of the reality of a 'centred-self'. The crucial importance of that reality, and the need to accept its mystery, is a major point in modern existential thinking (see 'Existentialism').

The notion of substance has been prominent in theological discussion of the sacrament of the Lord's Supper. We may refer to the doctrines of transubstantiation, and consubstantiation. Transubstantiation is the title of a Roman Catholic dogma, that is to say, teaching formulated by the Church to which assent must be given, on pain of excommunication. According to this dogma, when a priest pronounces the words of consecration of the elements of bread and wine, the substance of each of them is transformed into the body and blood of Jesus Christ, without any change whatever in the qualities of those elements. This dogma was rejected by the Protestant Reformers as a false and

67

superstitious interpretation of the fact of the Real Presence of Jesus Christ.

Consubstantiation is the name given to Lutheran teaching about what happens at the sacrament. Luther believed that Jesus in his humanity is omnipresent, now that he is "seated at the right hand of God". Therefore, he held, though the substance of bread and wine is not changed, Jesus himself is present bodily "in, with, and under" those elements (see 'Sacraments').

Substance has also had a central place in classical formulations of the doctrine of the Trinity. In trying to make clear, for example, that Jesus was completely divine, as well as human, theologians denied the view that Jesus was like the Father in substance (homoi-ousion, in Greek). For them, the only adequate expression was to say that Jesus Christ was of the same substance (homo-ousion) with the Father. The relation between the Father and the Son was therefore also described, in Latin form, as 'con-substantial'. This term is applied to all three members of the Trinity. (See also 'Christology', 'Trinity'.)

SYMBOL is sometimes used to describe an ecclesiastical creed, or confession of faith. So used, it retains its very ancient sense of 'a password'. Persons who are to be admitted into membership of a Church have to repeat, or acknowledge, the statement of faith which it has approved. The study of such creeds and confessions, in their historical setting, in their relation to one another, and in relation to contemporary beliefs, is a branch of theology called Symbolics.

Symbols, in that sense, are closely linked with Christian initiation, and therefore with Baptism and Holy Communion. An extension of meaning takes place, however, when the sacraments themselves are described as symbols. They are so described, because they signify and mediate a relationship between the worshippers and God.

With such usages in mind, it is helpful to make a distinction between symbols and emblems. A religious symbol is whatever, under God, awakens living faith, or is used to express living faith (see 'Faith'). Without this relationship of living faith, the same thing is a religious emblem. Thus, a cross may be a religious symbol, or it may be no more than an ornament associated with religion. What is an emblem for one person, may be a religious symbol for another. What was at one time a religious symbol may become, even for the same person, no more than an emblem.

This distinction becomes important in the discussion of verbal symbols. A verbal religious symbol does more than give some account of religious reality; it is a medium. For example, the parables of our Lord are sometimes treated as illustrations of religious truths. At the first, however, and ever since, they have been found to be more than that: they have awakened, enlarged, corrected, and transmitted faith in God. As such, they are verbal symbols of religion. (See also 'Analogy', 'Myth'.)

TELEOLOGICAL ARGUMENTS for the existence of God are also known as Arguments from Design. They rest on the fact of adaptation of means to ends, in the natural world. They assume that intelligent choice is a causative factor in the world as we know it. The argument, as put forward by Thomas Aquinas (about 1225–74), for example, runs as follows. In the world, there are things or beings which lack intelligence, but yet act for some purpose. They act always, or nearly always, so as to obtain the best result. Accident, or chance, is no explanation of this fact. Moreover, lacking intelligence, they could not of themselves fulfil a purpose. Therefore, they must be directed by some being who is endowed with knowledge and intelligence, as an arrow is shot to its mark by an archer. Some intelligent being exists, therefore, by whom all natural things are directed. This we call God.

This kind of argument has been severely criticized. Spinoza (1632–77) thought it was based on human imagination, and that the whole notion of means and ends was an insult to the perfection of God. (See also 'Ontology', 'Eternity'.) David Hume (1711–76) also thought it was a piece of unjustified reasoning from human experience of parts of the observable world, which could not possibly apply to the universe as a whole. It also overlooks the large number of purposeless happenings in the world. Even as it stands, he contended, the argument by no means leads to the conclusion that there is one, personal, supreme Being. The alleged facts could be accounted for if there were many gods, or even if the whole universe were an enormous animal or vegetable. Kant (1724–1804) pointed out that the argument did not deal with the 'matter', or 'substance', of the universe (see 'Substance'). Even if it were a sound piece of reasoning, therefore, it could lead only to a kind of architect of the universe, not a creator. An almighty architect could still be limited, to some extent, by the 'material' he was using. He could not be God, in the sense required by the argument.

Modern forms of the argument do not appeal to particular cases of adaptation to be found in the world. They take account of the bearing upon the argument of the theory of evolution. They are willing to acknowledge, also, the facts of waste in the world, and the apparent lack of design in parts of it. They do appeal, however, to the fact of a general orderliness in nature. The world in general is intelligible. The inorganic aspects of it serve the organic in a way which need not have been so. If the moral argument (which see) is joined with a modified version of the argument from design, then, it is urged, a strong and reasonable conviction of the existence of a supreme, intelligent Being as the author of the universe can be reached. In other words, along this line, as along others, no assent-compelling argument for the existence of God is possible. We do get, however, a number of considerations which point in the general direction of belief in God, as alone able to explain why anything is at all.

THEOLOGY is concerned with the nature, history, and validity of religious faith. It is especially, but not exclusively, the study of the history and truth of the beliefs in which such faith is expressed. This article is confined to Christian theology, which itself however (see below) takes other beliefs into account.

Theology is concerned with living faith to be found today in Christian communities, and with expressions of such living faith. For this reason, one qualification for studying theology is personal sharing in Christian faith. It is of course not only possible, but also important, for non-Christians to study Christian beliefs, practices, and institutions, as historical and contemporary factors in such fields as sociology, philosophy, ethics, economics, politics, culture, and the history of religions. Without some first-hand experience of God, however, the student of theology proper is as handicapped for the task as a person born blind, or born deaf, for the study of painting, or music.

If theology is concerned with present-day faith, it is with present-day faith as continuous with, a living heritage from, the faith of Christ's earliest disciples, which in turn has been transmitted by succeeding generations of Christians. Such faith is rooted in the conviction that, in Jesus Christ, God has uniquely made himself known, and given himself, to men for their salvation.

From this, it follows that the first part of theology consists in Biblical studies. The New Testament is the primary written witness to the nature and grounds of Christian faith at the first. The Old Testament must be studied, because of the way it was used by Jesus Christ himself, by his disciples, and by the Churches ever since. Intertestamental literature, including the Apocrypha found in some editions of the Bible, bears upon our understanding of the Old and the New Testaments. Biblical studies include the languages in which the books were written, textual criticism, literary problems – the date, authorship, and historical setting of each document. They also include the chronology, customs, cultures, and geography referred to in the Bible, or bearing upon it. The way in which the Bible as we have it came to be (what is

71

called the problem of the Canon of the Bible) must also be studied. Finally, making use of the results of other studies, there is the work of exegesis and interpretation.

The second part of theology is Church History. This includes the history of the spread of the Christian movement; the development of forms of worship, church organization and administration, relationships with civil society, and inter-church relations; and the history of doctrine, including the formulation of creeds and confessions of faith.

The third part is systematic theology – the comprehensive, coherent, critical, and contemporary study of Christian doctrine. It is based upon Biblical studies, and upon the history of doctrine. Its aim, however, is to expound Christian teaching in the light of two main problems, which present themselves in rather different form in each generation. The first arises from the fact that different Churches, and even different parties within the same Church, hold divergent, and sometimes mutually contradictory, beliefs. The second problem is due to the fact that Christian convictions are denied, or doubted, on grounds seriously and sincerely held by non-Christians. Systematic theology is, therefore, divided into two parts. In so far as it concentrates chiefly on the first problem, it may be called Dogmatics. In so far as it is directed mainly to the second problem, it is sometimes called Apologetics. In connection with both problems, an important part of the task of systematic theology is critical study of the ways in which words and phrases have been used in the past, and are being used today.

The fourth part of theology is the critical application of Christian doctrine to (1) the worship, organization, life and work of the Church itself, and (2) the problems of conduct, and the social issues, which confront its members. This part is sometimes called Practical Theology. It includes such studies as liturgics, homiletics, religious education, Church government, ecumenical relations, missions, pastoralia, and Christian ethics.

TRINITY – The doctrine of the Trinity is rooted in Biblical witness to the self-revelation of God. To meet serious differences in teaching, and consequent disunity, it was formulated in technical terms, and was incorporated in confessions of faith and creeds which were authorized, at various times, by both Catholic (Roman, and Eastern Orthodox) and Reformed Churches. In spite of that, the formal statement of the doctrine has been, and still is, interpreted in a variety of ways.

So far as Biblical witness is concerned, the Old Testament records both a wide variety of happenings which were interpreted as revelatory of God's nature and purposeful activity, and also manifold reflection upon them. In relation to our present subject, however, the living faith which was awakened by God's self-revelation expressed itself in the summary declaration: "Hear, O Israel, the Lord our God is one Lord" (Deut. 6: 4). This faith in the unity of God was shared by the first disciples of Jesus, and by members of the primitive Church. The New Testament, which makes this clear, also testifies that the early Christians were constrained to express their faith in Jesus as 'Lord'. This title, as we have just been reminded by the quotation from Deuteronomy, was often used by Jews for God (see 'Christology'). Such recognition of the unique relationship of Jesus Christ to God is expressed in a number of ways (cf. 2 Cor. 5: 19; Col. 2: 9; Heb. 1: 3; John 1: 1; 14: 9; 17: 5). Not only so, the New Testament witnesses to other happenings which were interpreted as revelatory of God, and explicitly linked with God's self-revelation both to Israel and in Jesus Christ; namely, the 'coming', or 'outpouring', and continuing activity, of the Holy Spirit (cf. Acts 2; 1 Cor. 12; Gal. 5: 22). New Testament statements on the Holy Spirit do not always seem consistent. Nevertheless, a tendency to distinguish the Holy Spirit from God the Father, and Jesus Christ as the Son, is plain enough. It forms a background to such explicit statements as the apostolic benediction (2 Cor. 13: 14), and the baptismal formula in St Matthew's Gospel (28: 19; see 'Holy Spirit').

The origins of trinitarian doctrine, then, are not to be found in

F

speculation, but in Biblical testimony to the self-communication of God, and to Christian response to it, and also in the experience of the early Church. It was under the pressure of controversy, however, that the formulation of the doctrine took the shape it did. It employed Greek and Latin terms, which were chosen to express as precisely as possible what the Church believed, and also to deny as firmly as possible those views which failed to do justice to its living faith. One classical formulation may be quoted, as representative of others. It was drawn up in Constantinople in 382 by "the orthodox bishops", and was addressed to bishops "assembled in the great city of Rome". "This is the faith which ought to be sufficient for you, for us, for all who wrest not the word of the true faith, for it is the ancient faith, it is the faith of our baptism, it is the faith that teaches us to believe in the name of the Father, of the Son, and of the Holy Spirit. According to this faith, there is one Godhead, Power, and Being of the Father, and of the Son, and of the Holy Spirit; the dignity being equal, and the majesty being equal in three perfect hypostases, i.e. three perfect persons."

This and similar formulations of faith in the triune God, how-ever carefully done, and however widely received, are neverthe-less bound to be in some measure unsatisfactory. The main reason is the mystery, the hiddenness, of the being of God, and the inadequacy of any terms to express even what man does apprehend of the living, self-communicating God (see 'Myth'). A secondary, but still important, reason is the constant need of later generations to interpret the language of their predecessors. Words (e.g. 'person', 'substance') change their significance. They take much of their meaning from contemporary ways of thinking and this varies from age to age.

The numerous attempts to interpret classical formulations of the doctrine of the Trinity tend to fall into one or other of three groups. First, those usually labelled modalist, or Sabellian (after Sabellius, third century). These emphasize the unity of God, but explain the 'three persons' as God's manifestation of himself successively as Father, Son, and Holy Spirit; or, as the threefold

74

way in which believers have experienced the self-communication of the one God. Second, those which emphasize the three persons, and explain the 'unity' of God in terms of their identical divine being (see 'Substance'). One in divine being, God exists eternally in three spheres of consciousness and activity – threefold in himself, and threefold in relation to the world and man (cf. the famous metaphor of Gregory of Nazianzus: 'one mingling of light, as it were of three suns joined together'). Third, those which use the analogy of personal society and complete fellowship. These also emphasize the three persons, but explain the 'unity' of God, less in terms of identical divine being, more in terms of organic unity.

UNIVERSALISM is the doctrine that, finally, all personal beings shall be saved through the sovereign mercy of God.

It is sometimes known as the doctrine of Restoration, or by the Greek word Apokatastasis (see Matt. 12: 11). Before it was officially condemned in the sixth century, leading Greek theologians taught universalism as an orthodox view. During the Middle Ages, it was associated with sectarian groups, and pietists. It has found serious support in more modern times.

In defence of the doctrine, some passages from Scripture have been quoted (e.g. Rom. 11: 32). Some which tell against it have been interpreted in a favourable sense: for example, Hell has been taken to be a state of further probation and purification by suffering. It would be generally agreed, however, that universalism cannot be established in these ways, but only by an appeal to the general drift of Christian doctrine as a whole.

The gracious, steadfast love of God towards all sinners is basic doctrine (see 'Justification by Faith'). That Jesus Christ suffered and died on behalf of all men, would also be generally agreed (see 'Atonement'). The doctrine of creation includes the belief that man is made for fellowship with God in his kingdom (see 'Imago Dei'). Moreover, the attitude of love towards all men, whoever they are and whatever their condition, is a mark of the

75

Christian who is reconciled to God (see 'Reconciliation'), and this suggests that no Christian could fully enjoy the blessedness of the saved, if any others were finally lost.

Over against these considerations is the insight of faith, responsive to God's self-manifestation, that salvation is essentially personal. In his sovereign and unwearied patience, God will undoubtedly continue to deal with that aspect of man's disobedience which is unwitting (see 'Sin'). The divine purpose for man, however, is expressible in terms of a divine community of persons. Even allowing for all the inadequacy of human speech in these matters, does not God's purpose require a personal response, in trust and obedience, before any man can be saved? What, then, of the person who in this life, and the next, continually turns away from what he knows of the gracious dealings of God with him? The upholder of universalism can only reply that, on the basis of New Testament teaching as a whole, it is to him unthinkable that God should finally fail to bring anyone to the point where he freely accepts the mercy of God. It is in this sense, he would go on to say, and not in the sense of God's overriding of the will of men, that he would understand the omnipotence of God. (See also 'Attributes of God', 'Predestination'.)

WORD OF GOD, while used in several ways, means essentially that God, who is infinite and would otherwise be entirely hidden from man, has expressed and does express himself. Word is to be understood in the general sense of 'utterance', a 'making outer', and therefore, in so far as it is intelligible, as a self-revealing. Such utterance is not, however, necessarily verbal: see, for example, Ps. 19: 1–4.

In theology, the 'Word of God' is used mainly in four ways. First, and primarily, it designates Christ as in his person and work the perfect expression of God. This usage implies convictions suggested, for example, in the Prologue to St John's Gospel, and developed doctrinally in Christology (which see). Second, it is applied to the Scriptures, as written testimony to God's self-revealing. Third, it is used in connection with the preaching of the Gospel. Fourth, but less frequently, it is applied to the sacraments. This fourfold use is sometimes distinguished as "the Word of God", "the Word of God written", "the Word of God preached", and "the Visible Word".

Much confusion arises from failure to recognize, or to state, that 'the Word of God written', 'the Word of God preached', and 'the Visible Word', are subordinate to, and agencies of 'the Word of God', but not simply identifiable with the Word. The Scriptures of the Old and New Testaments, for example, are often described as 'the Word of God'. Without further explanation, this might suggest that the words of the Bible, as they stand, are the words of God. The Bible is 'the Word of God written' when, through it, the reader is confronted with the living 'Word of God'. So it is with 'the Word of God preached', and 'the Visible Word'. (See further, 'Revelation', 'Holy Scripture', 'Sacraments').

INDEX

80